MANUAL

OF THE

EVIDENCES OF CHRISTIANITY,

FOR CLASSES AND PRIVATE READING.

BY

STEPHEN G. BULFINCH, D. D.

BOSTON:
WILLIAM V. SPENCER,
203 WASHINGTON STREET.
1866.

Stereotyped at the Boston Stereotype Foundry,

No. 4 Spring Lane.

TO

ANDREW P. PEABODY, D.D., LL.D.,

PLUMMER PROFESSOR OF CHRISTIAN MORALS
IN HARVARD UNIVERSITY,

This Work,

WHOSE PREPARATION HE HAS ENCOURAGED,

IS DEDICATED,

IN TOKEN OF RESPECT AND FRIENDSHIP,

BY THE AUTHOR.

CAMBRIDGE, MAY, 1866.

of the Gospels. For some further remarks upon this branch of his subject, the author would refer to his articles on the Tübingen school, in the Monthly Religious Magazine for January, February, and May of the present year. He is under obligation to several gentlemen who have furnished facilities for his work, and especially to President Hopkins, of Williams College, for permission to make use of his valuable "Lowell Lectures." From these he has derived important aid, particularly in the part entitled "The Christian System."

PREFACE.

It has been thought that, at the present time, when many reject altogether the claims of Christianity, and many who love and reverence it have very indefinite ideas regarding the authority with which it comes to us, a brief statement of the leading evidences of its divine origin might be acceptable and useful, not only to the private inquirer, but as a manual for public seminaries, and advanced classes in Sunday schools. In preparing this little work, the evidences have been carefully reëxamined, in the light of recent investigations in natural science and in theology. The book will be found to contain a brief examination of the principal theories that have been advanced, in Germany and elsewhere, for the explanation of the New Testament miracles, and of the doubts which have been suggested with regard to the authenticity

CONTENTS.

INTRODUCTORY.

THE CHRISTIAN SYSTEM.

THE AUTHOR OF CHRISTIANITY.

INSTITUTIONS OF CHRISTIANITY.

EVIDENCE OF THE RECORD.

I. EXTERNAL EVIDENCE.

II. INTERNAL EVIDENCE.

MODERN SPECULATIONS.

THE OLD TESTAMENT.

EVIDENCES OF CHRISTIANITY.

INTRODUCTORY.

SECTION 1. REVELATION.

THE knowledge which men possess with regard to religious subjects, is, generally speaking, traditional; that is, derived from those who went before them. But if we go farther back, and seek for the original sources of religious knowledge, there are only three that occur to us as conceivable. Religious ideas may be *innate* within the mind; they may be derived from the contemplation of *nature;* or they may be received from *revelation.*

Our innate ideas, or intuitive convictions, give evidence of the distinction between right and wrong, of the existence of some superior Power, and of our destiny to live hereafter.

Nature, or the order of God's works, confirms these truths, and assures us of the Unity, Benevolence, and other attributes of our Creator.

But notwithstanding these means of knowledge, men in various ages have fallen into most dangerous errors with regard to religion and morality. They have worshipped many gods, instead of one, and have supposed these beings to be limited in power and knowledge, stained with the grossest crimes, and only to be conciliated by the most degrading and unnatural services. From such errors great corruption and misery have proceeded.

Among the ancient heathen, morality became entirely separated from religion. The customs of society were debased by ferocity and licentiousness: witness the gladiatorial combats, and the open practice of impurities which cannot now even be named. Human sacrifices were sometimes offered, even in the most polished ages of Greece and Rome, and divine honors were paid to men and women of the most abandoned character.

Even now, in the most enlightened countries, those who reject Christianity are not agreed respecting some of the most important truths of what is called Natural Religion. Some deny the reality of a future life, and some the existence of a personal God.

Our innate ideas, and the contemplation of nature, are not sufficient, then, to impart the knowledge of religious truth. There appears, therefore, a probability that He who made us would give us further guidance on subjects of such importance. He created the human race for virtue and happiness; would he not interpose to rescue them when wandering in sin and misery? He imparted to them religious capacities and wants; would he not probably furnish the means for their gratification?

It may be added, that only by revelation could human

beings be assured of any personal interest felt in them by their Creator; the order of nature testifying only to his care for his creatures generally, or in masses. The ideas of God as hearing prayer, and as being ready to forgive and bless the individual worshipper, though they might be suggested by innate feeling, could be confirmed only by revelation.

The probability of a revelation having been made is confirmed by the very general belief of mankind that such has been the case; — a belief derived, probably, among heathen nations, from some dim tradition of a primitive divine communication.

Section 2. Miracle.

A miracle is an occurrence produced by superhuman power, in a manner different from the common course of nature.

Revelation, being distinguished from the teaching of nature, is necessarily miraculous. It may or may not be accompanied by outward miracles; but if it is extraordinary, — occurring once only, or at intervals in the history of the world, — it is itself a miracle, by the definition given above. It would be as truly a miracle for God to interfere with the common laws of mind as with those of matter. To deny, then, the possibility of miracle is to deny the possibility that God should ever make a revelation to his creatures.

It is true that the order of nature is marked by beautiful consistency and uniformity; and no departure from it can be supposed to have taken place, but for the most important reasons. Yet miracles are not incredible, because, —

1. The power of God to produce them is infinite.

2. The communication of religious knowledge, involving the principles by which life is to be guided, and happiness secured, here and hereafter, is an object of such high importance, that it seems worthy of miraculous intervention.

3. Science testifies that miracles have been performed. The creation was a miracle, or rather a succession of miracles. The world itself bears witness to the action of its Author, at some former time or times, in a manner different from his usual action by what are called the laws of nature. Geology teaches that the earth, for a long succession of ages, was in a condition in which life neither did nor could exist. It testifies, also, that different forms of vegetable and animal life were produced at successive periods, as the earth was fitted to receive them. In every such production the action of the Almighty was different from the common course of nature. That course is to preserve and to propagate; the action in these instances was to create. These, therefore, were miracles.

Some have imagined that the existing variety of animal and vegetable life was the result of gradual development of complicated forms from those more simple. If this were true, the number of miracles would be less, but the fact of miraculous creation must still be admitted, to account for the existence of those simple forms.

Even if this theory were maintained to the extravagant extent of supposing all forms of life to have sprung from "monads," or microscopic insects, — these to have been produced by spontaneous generation, — and, finally, the world itself, and the whole solar system, to have resulted from a rotatory motion in a mass of "nebulous" or chaotic matter, — still the action of almighty power in giving that first impulse must be recognized as a miracle. All that would be gained by so wild a conjecture would be to reduce the miracles of creation to one; and that one, being entirely exceptional, would be more directly contrary to the majestic order and gradual progress which the course of nature exhibits, than would a series of creative touches from the divine hand.

Miracles, then, have taken place in creation. It is not incredible, therefore, that they have occurred since. If God thus interposed, at successive periods, to bring into being the various forms of vegetable, animal, and human life, he may have interposed, at successive periods since, to communicate his will to his human offspring. This, as we believe, he did, in the primitive, the Jewish, and the Christian revelations.

4. Miracles may be consistent with laws of nature unknown to us.

A bird which has always lived in a forest, and has never seen a human being, finds, on returning to seek its nest at night, that the tree which bore it is prostrate, although there has been no storm. This is a miracle to the bird; it is out of the course of nature to which the bird has been accustomed. To us it is no miracle; it is simply that a settler has cut down the tree. The interference, then, of a superior being, or order of beings, with an inferior, may produce a miracle to the latter; yet it may be perfectly consistent with the laws of the superior being's nature.

To take another illustration: The sun rises every

day, the comet becomes visible perhaps once in a thousand years; yet the appearance of the comet is in accordance with the laws of nature as truly as the rising of the sun. So the manifestation, at long intervals, of creative power in geologic epochs, or of spiritually renewing and wonder-working power in successive revelations, may be in conformity to laws as firmly established and as sublime as that of gravitation.

It has been contended that all human experience testifies against miracles. Our individual experience can count for very little, from the limited range of our observation; and the experience of ages past is known to us only by the testimony of those who then lived. Some of these — the sacred writers — expressly declare that miracles took place. Others are silent respecting them; but no one directly contradicts, from his own knowledge, the assertion of the sacred writers. Here, then, is only testimony against testimony; nay, testimony which is merely neutral against that which is positive.

Miracles, however, are confessedly events of very rare occurrence. We know of but two purposes to which they are applied — creation and revelation. The reason is obvious: every other purpose of divine Providence is best accomplished by the common order of the universe, but these two imply miracle in their very nature. To command our belief, miracles must meet the following conditions: —

1. They must be, in themselves, worthy of a divine origin. The miracles wrought by the Savior were dignified, and, in general, directly beneficent in their character.

2. The revelation they are wrought to establish must

be worthy of our reception. No amount of alleged miraculous evidence could sustain doctrines dishonorable to God, or inconsistent with pure morality.

3. They must be proved by satisfactory evidence; such, for example, as the testimony of several intelligent eye-witnesses, given independently of each other, and under circumstances which showed that they had neither been bribed nor deluded.

The Christian religion expressly claims to have been accompanied by miracles. (Mark xvi. 17, 20; John x. 25, 37, 38; Acts ii. 22, 32.) We cannot consistently receive it as true, and yet reject its claims in this important particular.

Even if Christianity should be received as our guide, on account of the self-evident truth of its instructions, still its miracles would not be superfluous. They would mark it as being not a discovery of man, but a revelation from God, possessing authority that entitles it to obedience, and expressing the love of the Creator, as a personal message from a father expresses his love to his children.

The question, however, most suitable for the inquirer into the truth of Christianity, is not whether it was best that God should reveal his will miraculously, but whether he has actually done so.

THE CHRISTIAN SYSTEM.

SECTION 3. CHRISTIANITY AT FIRST VIEW.

THE inquiry now presents itself, Is the Christian religion worthy of the divine origin it claims? Some facts respecting it meet us at the first glance.

1. It is the religion of the most enlightened portion of the world. Christianity and civilization go together; and the freest and most advanced countries are those in which this religion is held in its purest form. Where the gospel has prevailed, science and art have flourished, and institutions of learning and charity have been maintained, which before its introduction were unknown.

2. The condition of woman has been more elevated and happy in Christian lands than in others. In Turkey, woman is a prisoner; in India, a slave and a victim.

3. The greatest men, in intellectual and moral endowments, have usually been among the foremost in their acknowledgment of Christianity; and, generally speaking, the most honest men, the most useful citizens, the firmest friends, and the most liberal benefactors, have been decided Christians.

4. The excellence of Christianity has been admitted by many even of those who did not believe in its authority; and those sceptics who have led virtuous lives have generally been those who had been brought up in Christian homes.

5. While systems of human philosophy have been improved through successive generations after the death of their founders, Christianity stands in its best form as displayed in its original documents. Endeavors to improve it have merely resulted in corrupting it; and attempts to reform it find success only as they bring it back to "the simplicity that is in Christ."

6. When we look at the religion itself, we perceive that it gives the most exalted ideas of God, — as One, Infinite, and Eternal; as Holy, Just, and Merciful.

7. It gives, also, the most correct ideas of man, — as possessed of great capacities and powers, and destined for noble purposes; but as led away by sin, and needing repentance and amendment.

8. It gives rational and elevated ideas of human duty, as comprised in self-control, usefulness, and piety. Its morality is not only elevated, but strict, guarding thought as well as action.

9. It gives a lofty view of man's final destiny, representing him as designed by his Maker for immortal life and happiness.

10. The Christian religion, and that alone, exhibits a fitness to become universal. Other systems are limited by their peculiarities to the region of their birth. Mohammedanism insists on various ablutions, healthful and agreeable in warm countries, but not adapted to colder regions. Judaism, though divine in its origin, was not designed for universal acceptance until completed by Christianity. It required all males to present themselves three times a year at the Temple, which was the only one permitted to be built. This, and numerous other restrictions, marked it as a national religion.

(Exodus xxiii. 17; Deut. xii. 13, 14.) But Christianity gives the command, "Preach to every creature" (Mark xvi. 15), and its character and institutions are consistent with that command. Christ came to save his people, not from the Roman yoke, which would have been a local and temporary object, but "from their sins," an object of universal character. (Matt. i. 21.)

Section 4. Comparison with other Religions, continued.

The other religions in the world are Judaism, Mohammedanism, Buddhism, Heathenism in its various forms, and Deism.

Judaism, the religion of the Old Testament, was given as preparatory to Christianity; is acknowledged by it as of divine origin, and is, to a great extent, included in it. It is not complete in itself. (Heb. xi. 39, 40.) It does not, as distinctly as Christianity, represent the Supreme Being as the impartial Father of all mankind; does not as strongly impress the obligation of some duties, — that of mercy, for instance; and does not as clearly teach the doctrine of a future life.

The sublimity of the Christian ideas of God is more observable when contrasted with the narrow spirit of the Jews near the period at which Jesus lived. The author of the Second Book of Esdras, in the Apocrypha, apparently a half Christianized Jew, uses the following language: "O Lord, thou madst the world for our sakes. As for the other people, which also come of Adam, thou hast said that they are nothing." (2 Esdras

vi. 55, 56.) Contrast with this the Savior's recognition of the brotherhood of all mankind. (Matt. v. 43–45; Luke x. 27–37; John x. 16.)

Mohammedanism is only a corruption of Judaism and Christianity. With many excellent precepts, derived from these, it combines many harsh commands and formal observances. Contrary to the pure and peaceful character of Christianity, it places little restraint on sensuality, and encourages the stern, warlike, and ambitious spirit, rather than the gentle and forgiving. Its inferiority is the more marked, as, coming later than Christianity, it might have been expected to have improved upon it.

The corrupted form of Christianity called Mormonism strongly resembles Mohammedanism in the particulars just mentioned, and affords a striking illustration of the excellence of Christianity, by the miserable failure of the attempt to improve it.

Buddhism may be properly distinguished from other forms of heathenism, both on account of its extensive prevalence, and as being more properly atheistic than polytheistic. It denies the existence of an eternal God, gives imperfect rules of human duty, and makes the highest happiness consist in the extinction of our personal being.

Heathenism, in all its forms, is full of ideas and practices dishonorable to God and degrading to man.

In ancient heathen nations there were great philosophers who rose above their religion and their age, and taught many exalted lessons of virtue; but they did not derive the sanction for it from the hope or fear of a future life. Plato, in one remarkable passage of the

Phædon, describes Socrates as speaking as a Christian might speak; but the instance is a solitary one. Generally, the heathen writers speak of the future life in uncertain language, or describe it in an unattractive aspect; and seldom appeal to considerations connected with it, to enforce the obligations of morality.

Neither Mohammedanism, Buddhism, nor any form of heathenism, has any claim to rest on the evidence of miracles. Mohammed disclaimed miracles as proofs of his system, telling his followers that the Koran itself was a miracle. There are some miraculous stories told respecting him, as that of his night journey to heaven on the horse Alborak; but they rest only on his own word, not having been witnessed by any other person.

The wonders of Brahminism, and those of ancient heathenism, are alleged to have taken place in far distant ages, before the rise of authentic history. They rest on the word of poets, not of historians.

If Deism be proposed to take the place of Christianity, under the more specious name of Theism, or the Religion of Nature, it may be observed that the doctrines usually supposed to constitute this system are mostly derived from the gospel. The modern Deist, born of Christian parents, and subjected in youth and manhood to the influences of Christian instruction and society, combines the best ideas he has received, and excluding from his spiritual temple the foundation of faith in Christ, calls the beautiful but now baseless structure the Religion of Nature. Men are so accustomed to the thought of God's unity, infinity, and goodness, and to the doctrine of a future life, that they forget how much they are indebted, even for these truths, to the Bible.

And notwithstanding the advantage of Christ's teaching, those who discard his authority are not agreed with regard to many of the most important subjects, such even as the existence of a personal God as distinct from nature, and the hope of a future life to the individual as distinct from the continued existence of the race to which he belongs.

SECTION 5. CHRISTIANITY IN HARMONY WITH NATURE.

Among the works of God a degree of harmony may justly be expected, either in resemblance or in adaptation to each other. This harmony exists between nature and Christianity.

Christianity coincides with the highest teachings of natural religion, in the exalted view it gives of the divine nature and attributes. And this harmony is the more apparent as the teachings of nature have been interpreted by science, proving the immense extent of creation, and that all portions of it are under the control of the same grand system of laws. These discoveries correspond to what the Bible taught long before, of the unity of God, and his unbounded power, wisdom, and love.

God's moral government, as displayed by Christianity, is analogous to his government over outward nature. The power of gravitation acts not only on large bodies, but on small; not only on masses, but on atoms. So in God's moral government, the laws of right and wrong are applicable to the least of our actions as to the greatest; and Christ tells us, "Every idle word that men shall speak they shall give account thereof in the day of judgment." (Matt. xii. 36.)

Nature and Christianity alike teach most clearly what is of practical importance, leaving theoretical truth for subsequent discovery. Thus natural instinct prompts to use the day for labor and the night for rest; but men did not discover for ages what it was that produced this interchange of light and darkness. So Christianity teaches the great practical doctrine of a future state; but how that state will be constituted is not explained. Mohammedanism, on the contrary, enters into a minute, and often an absurd, description of the realms of bliss and of woe.

The operation of Christianity upon the heart of man, and upon the institutions of society, is generally gradual, like the changes produced in nature. "First the blade, then the ear, after that the full corn in the ear." (Mark iv. 28.) In its remedial character it is analogous to other remedies, often, like them, requiring of its patients self-restraint and self-denial.

In its mediatorial character, too, it is analogous to nature. To save another from evil, it is necessary that we take some labor or pain upon ourselves. The sick child is saved by the sleepless care of the mother; the endangered country by its soldiers, faithful unto death; the neglected prisoners by the self-sacrifice of the philanthropist. The death of Christ for our salvation is, then, in harmony with a universal law.

The agreement of Christianity with nature has been made use of as an argument against its claims. It is said by some that the teachings of Christ are, in what is most important, only repetitions of moral and religious lessons that had been given before. Efforts have been made to prove this with respect to the Lord's Prayer (Matt. vi. 9) and the Golden Rule. (Matt. vii. 12.) The reply is, that, of course, if the principles taught by Christ were eternal truth, they could not be new; if they were truth of the highest importance, God would not have left the world for ages entirely without them. Many of the teachings of Jesus, therefore, had very probably been anticipated by those before his time. But he came, not so much to declare what was entirely new, as to give the most important religious and moral truth to mankind, in a connected form, free from human error, and with the authoritative sanction of a revelation; and by his example, his death and resurrection, to illustrate the whole system, and make it effectual for the salvation of mankind.

Section 6. Christianity adapted to Man.

The harmony of the Christian religion with the system of divine government manifested in nature may be further seen in its adaptation to the various powers and capacities of man.

It is adapted to the intellect and the imagination; for it presents to the former the loftiest themes of contemplation, and kindles the latter by its representations of beauty and grandeur. Not to speak at present of the lofty poetry of the Old Testament, it is sufficient to refer to the parables of the Good Samaritan (Luke x.) and the Prodigal Son (Luke xv.); to the discourse with the woman of Samaria (John iv.), to the portraiture of Charity (1 Cor. xiii.), and the chapter on the resurrection (1 Cor. xv.), with the description of the final judgment. (Rev. xx. 11, 12.)

It is adapted to the conscience and the will; for it holds before the mind the claims of duty, not on the ground of expediency alone, but on that of God's appointment. It declares the way of virtue to be the way even of earthly happiness, pointing out the rewards which attend it, and ascribing them to the wise providence of God. (Matt. v.; 1 Tim. iv. 8.) It denounces, in his name, corresponding penalties against transgression. (Matt. v. 21–26.) Still more, it assures us that the reward of virtue and the penalty of guilt will be extended beyond this world, teaching us to expect a righteous judgment. (Matt. xxv.; Rom. ii. 5–10.) By the strictness of its moral requirements, it excites the conscience, alarming us with a view of our condition in the sight of God. (Rom. iii. 19, 20, 23.) Yet it encourages us with the hope of pardon for the past, and divine assistance for the future. (Luke xi. 13; xviii. 13, 14; 1 John i. 9.)

It is adapted to the affections; for it places before us the highest object to which they can be directed — the infinitely good and holy Being, whom it presents to us as "our Father in heaven." (Matt. vi. 9; xxii. 37; 1 John iv. 8.) It displays the resemblance of his perfections in a human form in the Lord Jesus Christ, whose self-sacrificing labors and sufferings for our sake, endured with unexampled patience, dignity, and devotion to God, have proved the most effectual means to touch the heart. (John xii. 32; Heb. i. 3; ii. 10.) And it encourages the domestic and social affections, making love its great principle of action, and enforcing it by the example of the Savior. (Matt. xxii. 35–40; John xv. 12; Rom. xiii. 10; 1 John iv. 20, 21.)

Section 7. The Morality of Christianity.

By its adaptation to the conscience, the affections, and the will, Christianity commends and enforces its moral instructions. We have next to observe what is the character of these.

They comprise, in the first place, the law of right, the great principles of justice, purity, and benevolence. These, which wise men had in part discerned, are more fully given in the Old Testament, but in their perfection only by the Savior. (Exodus xx.; Matt. v. 17, 18; Rom. ii. 14.) The various manifestations of God's law, in nature, in the Old Testament and in the New, are thus harmonious.

The Christian law of morality comprises also some rules to which neither heathen wisdom nor Jewish inspiration had attained. These are sometimes directly given, as the limitation of anger (Matt. v. 21, 22), and of divorces (Matt. v. 31; Mark x. 2–9); and sometimes they are clearly implied; as polygamy and suicide, though nowhere directly forbidden, are evidently contrary, the one to the Christian duty of purity, the other to that of patient and faithful continuance in the service of God.

The Christian law is distinguished by the restraint which it places upon the propensities and passions. It forbids the exercise of malevolent feelings. Revenge, which among the heathen was regarded as the mark of a noble mind, is prohibited by Christianity. (Rom. xii.

19, 20.) Avarice, pride, vanity, and sensuality are alike forbidden. (Luke xii. 15; 1 John ii. 16.)

At the same time it avoids the extreme into which other systems have fallen, which have attempted to restrain the passions — that of a gloomy asceticism. (Matt. xi. 19; 1 Tim. iv. 4.)

Among the virtues there are some which have attracted the admiration of mankind in every age, and which were held in high honor alike by Jews and heathen at the time of the Savior. Such are active courage, friendship, and patriotism. There are others to which less of popular favor has been given, but which are no less important to human happiness, and in themselves no less worthy. Such are meekness, patience, forgiveness. The former class are in accordance with the natural impulses, the latter imply their restraint. An uninspired moralist would have advocated the popular virtues more than the unpopular, because he would have shared the popular feeling. An ambitious leader would have pursued a similar course, because he would have expected thus to gain favor. But Jesus gave his influence for the unpopular virtues, commending a meek, yielding, and peaceable course of conduct, directing us to love our enemies, and to return good for evil — precepts which would appear impracticable if his own example had not illustrated them. (Luke xxiii. 34; 1 Peter ii. 21–23.) This course showed at once his divine wisdom in enforcing those virtues which most needed commendation, and his superiority to all attempts to gain popular favor, while it renders the success of his religion the more wonderful. (Matt. v. 1–12, 38–48.)

It has been erroneously argued, even by some defenders of Christianity, that the Savior, in thus doing, discountenanced the manly virtues — courage, friendship, and patriotism. But this is going beyond the truth. He did not expressly commend these virtues, because they needed no commendation, being already favorites with the world; but he inculcated the principles from which they must proceed — reverence for God rather than man, which is the source of true courage; and love, of which friendship and patriotism are only applications. (Matt. xxii. 39; Luke xii. 4, 5; John xv. 12.)

Christianity goes deep into the cause of existing evils in society, and thus directs efforts more effectually to their removal. It does not ascribe these evils to the constitution of society, to defective institutions, to deficiency of wealth, or superabundance of population, but to sin; and it comes to free mankind from this evil. Other reformers have endeavored to remove particular forms of suffering and wrong, and have thus often done well, carrying out various portions of the great design of Christianity; but the gospel itself strikes at the root of all, representing the original evil of all to be man's disobedience to the divine law, and directing its strongest efforts to remove this. (Matt. xv. 18; Luke vi. 43.) This is not the ground which a fanatic would have taken; for honest enthusiasm, excited by the view of visible wrongs, would have attacked them directly; nor could such ground be taken by an impostor, the loftiest moral truth being discovered by one who himself was utterly untrue.

This aim of Christianity to remove the evil within, as the great means for the removal of all outward evil, presents an answer to those who defend any form of wrong — as slavery, for instance — by asserting that it is not forbidden by Christ; and also to those who consider his omitting to forbid it as furnishing an argument against his system. He did not undertake to specify the various forms of moral evil. He said nothing directly against despotism; nor did his apostles denounce the bloody gladiatorial combats, the favorite amusement of the heathen around them. But Christ and his disciples alike, aiming to subject the heart to the divine law, inculcated great principles, the most comprehensive of all being the love of God and man. Every institution and practice inconsistent with these is condemned by Christianity, and either has yielded or must yield to its influence. (Matt. v. 48; vii. 12; xxii. 37–40.)

It may be said, however, that, excellent as is the morality of the Christian system, its excellence does not oblige us to receive the religion; for that moral precepts claim to be obeyed for their own evident truth and beauty. If we found a good precept in the Koran, we might adopt it without believing in Mohammed; so we can use the moral commands of Jesus without believing in his divine commission. To this we reply, —

1. One who sincerely endeavors to obey the law of Christ for its intrinsic excellence will probably soon be convinced of his superhuman claims. (John vii. 17.)

2. No merely human wisdom could have originated so holy a system; or, if it could, those who were pure and exalted enough to invent it must have been superior to deception; and if the account of its first preachers be true, the system is divine. (1 John iv. 14.)

3. The morality of Christianity is inseparably connected with its religious teaching. Its philanthropy

proceeds from the love of God; its courage from the reverence due to him. (Matt. v. 44, 45; x. 28.)

The character of the Savior's teachings is well described in the following words of Professor Norton: "In the midst of men gross, sensual, uninformed, and unprincipled, his morality is the most pure, correct, and sublime; his views of duty are the most rational and comprehensive. Not only does he transcend, beyond all comparison, the rulers and teachers of his own nation, but it is the highest praise of the philosophers of ancient times, of Socrates and of Cicero, that their notions of religion and duty have some imperfect resemblance to those of Jesus of Nazareth." (Internal Evidences, pp. 308, 309.)

THE AUTHOR OF CHRISTIANITY.

SECTION 8. CHARACTER OF JESUS.

WE have next to consider the character of the person through whom the revelation was made. In most systems the personal character of the founder is comparatively of little importance. The works of Plato command admiration from the intellectual greatness they display — not from the moral qualities of the writer. Even the laws of Moses derive their sanction in a very slight degree from the personal character of the great lawgiver. But when a teacher claims the *love* of his followers, he must display those qualities by which love is won. This claim is made by the Author of Christianity. He calls his disciples friends; he requires them to commemorate him by a personal act of affection. (Matt. xii. 50; xxvi. 26; John xv. 14.) Neither a fanatic nor an impostor would have been likely to do this; for the feelings of the one would have been exclusively engaged on the object of his enthusiasm, and the other would have been without genuine feeling.

Those who do not receive Christianity as divinely revealed have often admitted the moral excellence of the Savior's character. Rousseau declared that "Socrates died like a philosopher, but Jesus Christ like a god;" and Renan declares, "Whatever may be the surprises of the future, Jesus will never be surpassed. His worship will grow young without ceasing; his legend will call forth tears without end; his sufferings will melt the noblest hearts; all ages will proclaim that among the sons of men there is none born greater than Jesus."

The character of the Savior, as presented by the evangelists, combines the strength of man with the tenderness of woman. He is faithful to every duty; and the virtues of the citizen, the friend, and the son, including some which his religion has been wrongly supposed to depreciate, are all rightly balanced. (See before, p. 19; see also Luke xix. 41–44; John xiii. 23; xix. 27.) He has courage to reprove most sternly, and gentleness to speak forgiveness to the penitent. (Matt. xxiii. 13–36; John viii. 11.) While going about doing good, and superior to all narrow prejudices of race or nation, he yet sets a limit to his own action and that of his disciples, lest their efforts should be wasted over too wide a field. (Matt. iv. 23; x. 5; xv. 24; Luke x. 30–37.) Denouncing the hypocrisy of the Pharisees, and preparing for the abrogation of the ceremonial law, he yet pays it respect while it remains in force. (Matt. viii. 4; xxiii. 2.) Forbidding avarice, and censuring the faults of the rich and powerful, he teaches the poor and oppressed lessons of patience and faith, and refuses to intermeddle with the distribution of property. (Matt. v.; Luke xii. 14.) He makes claim to the highest dignity, yet simply and unaffectedly; and without impairing his dignity, he performs a menial office when he can thereby teach an important lesson. (John xiii. 1–5.) He calls all men to come to him; yet, instead of using flattering persuasions, warns them that they will encounter obloquy and persecution. (Matt. xi. 28; Luke xxi. 12–16.)

But it is as the period of his suffering draws nigh that the beauty of his character most fully appears. The wise and tender counsels to his friends (John xiii.–xvi.), the prayer with his disciples (xvii.), the struggle with himself in Gethsemane (Matt. xxvi. 39), the dignity with which he meets his captors, asking only that his disciples may be spared (John xviii. 4, 8), the patience he shows under the abuse of the Sanhedrim (John xviii. 23), the look that brings repentance to the disciple who has denied him (Luke xxii. 61), the answers and the bearing that almost subdue the pride and policy of the Roman governor (John xviii. 33–38), — these prepare us for the still higher sublimity of the cross. Here we see him praying for the pardon of his enemies, and urging the only plea that could be available for them (Luke xxiii. 34); in his own agony, showing mercy to the penitent thief (43), and love and consideration for his mother (John xix. 26), and with his last breath commending his soul to God. (Luke xxiii. 46.)

If this holiest of all characters did not exist, whence came its delineation? It is one of the highest achievements of art to represent a perfect human *form;* what, then, must the artist be that could portray a perfect human *soul?* Writers of fiction seldom, if ever, create incidents; they merely vary and combine incidents from real life; and the occurrences which have been here presented had no prototype except in Jesus himself. The prayer for his murderers has often been imitated by his followers (Acts vii. 60), but it was first uttered by himself; and the more than royal exercise of mercy, from a cross instead of a throne (Luke xxiii. 43), was unexampled in the history of the world.

This argument is thus strongly presented in a manuscript sermon by the present President of Harvard College: —

"What wonderful, what superhuman genius is this, in this obscure Jew Matthew, that he should conceive of the office and work of a Messiah, never having heard of any Messiah except as an expected king and warrior; that he should draw the picture of one claiming to have come from God, claiming to be the future judge of the quick and the dead, claiming to be living in the bosom of God, — and draw the picture with such majesty and grace that it has commanded the admiration and implicit faith of all succeeding ages. In moral and intellectual character, Jesus is drawn in such fair and beautiful lines in the Gospels, that you can scarce conceive it within the possibilities of human genius to have invented the character. But when you add to this moral worth and intellectual power the claim to divine origin and divine authority, and find these immeasurable claims of Jesus so sweetly blended with humility that the reader detects no incongruity whatever, you have then a portrait which no human genius ever could, as it seems to me, have invented, and which certainly no human pencil could have drawn, had not the original been a living man."

Section 9. Position, Claims, and Success of Jesus.

The position, the claims, and the success of the Savior, taken together, present a proof in favor of his religion which may well be called a moral miracle. Eighteen centuries since, there was manifested among men a new moral power which changed the habits of thinking and acting among mankind, and advanced the race in all that was worthy of pursuit far more than all the teachings of philosophy had done. This great spiritual revolution came from a teacher in the obscure province of Galilee; humanly speaking, a poor young man, with few advantages, rejected by his own nation, and put to death, at their instance, by the Romans, who ruled them. Yet this poor and suffering teacher has subdued the civilized world. Perceiving this wonder, we easily assent to the outward miracles which accompanied it; nay, we receive them as necessary to account for this.

Let us notice his position, in contrast with his claims. Jesus was born in humble circumstances (Matt. xiii. 55); he possessed no literary advantages (John vii. 15), and derived his support, while teaching, from the contributions of friends. (Luke viii. 3.) His cause had not, therefore, the attractions of worldly power, but won its way in despite of an opposition which had on its side the force of wealth, rank, and national favor. (Matt. viii. 20; John vii. 48.) Yet the greatness of his claims is unexampled. He claimed miraculous power (John x. 25); he asserted that he always did what was pleasing to God. (John viii. 29.) He allowed himself to be called the Son of David. (Matt. xxi. 16.) He declared himself the promised Messiah (Matt. xvi. 17; John iv. 26), and that in him the prophecies were fulfilled. (Luke iv. 21; xxiv. 27.) He asserted that he was the Son of God (John x. 36), and, in some sense, one with the Father. (John x. 30.) He foretold that he should rise from the dead (Luke xviii. 33), and declared that he should hereafter judge the world. (Matt. xxv. 31; John v. 29.) He announced himself as "the light of the world" (John viii. 12), "the resurrection and the life." (John xi. 25.) If he was not divinely commissioned, he was guilty of the most audacious blasphemy, or he was insane. Yet these stupendous claims were advanced with calmness, and often implied rather than expressed, as if with a quiet assurance of their truth. (Matt. xix. 28.) With these claims he united a plan of spiritual conquest surpassing the wildest dreams of earthly ambition; yet he knew, and foretold, his own approaching fate. (Matt. xx. 17–19; xxi. 38, 39.) But, instead of being discouraged by this, he foresaw in his death the means for the triumph of his cause. (John xii. 32.) Such confidence would imply, in a merely uninspired man, the wildest self-delusion; but the dignity of his demeanor, and the practical good sense of his precepts, contradict the supposition. As to that of imposture, it cannot be entertained a moment.

With this unfavorable position, and these lofty claims, the course pursued by this teacher was the most unlikely to win popular favor. The Jews were at that time divided into three sects — the Pharisees, Sadducees, and Essenes. Jesus denounced the formalism and hypocrisy of the Pharisees; he differed from the unscriptural views and lax morality of the Sadducees (Matt. xxii. 23–30); and did not sanction the asceticism, the celibacy, and community of goods of the Essenes. (Matt. xi. 19; xix. 4, 11; Luke xii. 13, 14.) The one feeling which all had in common — that of national pride — he stirred up against himself. A fanatic would have *shared* this feeling, an impostor would have *made use* of it; he, on the contrary, set morality above ceremonies (Matt. xii. 1–13), associated with publicans (Matt. ix. 10), commended Samaritans (Luke x. 33; xvii. 16–19), and foretold the destruction of the holy city and temple. (Matt. xxiv. 2; xxii. 7.) And, while thus alienating the Jews, he did not seek the aid of the Gentiles. (Matt. xv. 24.) Yet he succeeded in establishing his system as the religion of the civilized world.

Let the rapidity of its progress be observed. The disciples of Jesus rallied in Jerusalem after their Master's crucifixion, and in the midst of his enemies. The first day's public preaching is said to have gained three thousand converts. (Acts ii. 41.) Persecution scattered them, but only to spread their sentiments more widely. (Acts viii. 1, 4.) At length they provoked a contest with the idolatry of the age, sustained by all the power of that empire which was then coëxtensive with the civilized world. Against all that power Christianity prevailed. The Roman empire fell, but its barbarian conquerors were subdued by the gospel. And now it is extending its outward conquests, it is purifying itself from corruptions of human device, and it is manifesting its power in the removal of evil institutions and customs. Such have been, and such are, the achievements of a system which its opponents would have us believe is but a collection of doubtful legends respecting a young carpenter of Galilee, and the fishermen, his associates!

SECTION 10. DEATH AND RESURRECTION OF JESUS.

The death and resurrection of Jesus are events which rest not alone upon the testimony of the New Testament historians. They must have taken place, in order to account for the existence of Christianity at the present time.

Some of the most important facts of Christianity are of such a character as never would have been invented by a writer friendly to its claims; besides which, they were in their nature facts of general notoriety. Such are the birth of Jesus in a lowly station, his rejection by his countrymen generally, and his execution as a criminal.

That Jesus died on the cross, we are assured by the unquestioned tradition, not only of the Christian church, but of its opponents. No heathen or Jewish writer ever denied the fact. This assurance, too, is confirmed by the nature of the case. He who undertakes the course of a reformer, and who exposes the vices of the leading classes, necessarily incurs their hatred. He who, with such a course, combines the claim to a divine commission, must either rule or perish. Unless his claim is allowed, the animosity it excites will be satisfied only by destroying him, as an impostor. The claims of Jesus were rejected by his nation: this we know, for that nation still rejects them. His execution, then, might be inferred as most highly probable, even if we possessed no record of it as a fact.

It will not, then, be questioned that Jesus was crucified — a mode of execution most painful, and, as then considered, most disgraceful. The triumph of his enemies was complete.

How, then, can the present existence of his religion be accounted for? What gave his followers — terrified and scattered as they must have been — courage to assemble again, and confidence in a cause which had been thus signally defeated, so that they commenced and carried forward the bold and active measures that were necessary to make it successful?

The resurrection of Jesus alone can answer these questions. This was early proclaimed as the great fact of the religion. Such is the testimony of the book of Acts, which must be admitted to be at least the earliest and best account of the apostles' preaching that we have. (Acts ii. 24, 32; iii. 15; xvii. 31; xxv. 19.) Such has been the unvarying testimony of the church from that time to the present.

Such is the testimony, among many others, of the First Epistle to the Corinthians (xv. 4, 14, 15, 20, 23), respecting which the ablest of modern sceptics makes the following remarkable admission: "This conclusion, however, does not shake the passage in the First Epistle to the Corinthians, which (it being undoubtedly genuine) was written about the year 59 after Christ, consequently not thirty years after his resurrection. On this authority we must believe that many members of the primitive church, who were yet living at the time when this Epistle was written, — especially the apostles, — were convinced that they had witnessed appearances of the risen Christ." (Strauss's Life of Jesus, Part III. chap. iv. § 138; first German edition, § 134.)

If Jesus was not divinely commissioned, there must have been a follower of his of genius equal to his own.

For the very foundation of Christianity is in the death and resurrection of Christ; and if he did not rise from the dead, it is impossible that he should build on these himself. Who, then, was it, that, after the death of Jesus, remodelled his teaching, rallied his disciples, and induced them to stand firm, even to the death? What a great man! and what a madman! The cross was ignominious; he tried to make men believe a crucified Jew the king of the world; and he succeeded!

The mode by which modern scepticism meets this argument is twofold. Some have fancied that Jesus did not really die, but was resuscitated by careful treatment. This theory will be examined hereafter; at present we only remark that it would not explain the resurrection of his religion. If Jesus, after enduring all the pain and shame of crucifixion, had been brought back to consciousness by human means, he could not have had either physical strength or mental confidence to resume the task of leadership; and the depression of his disciples would not have been changed to animation and courage by his recovery, if it had not implied a divine interposition.

On the other hand, Strauss, believing that Jesus actually died on the cross, explains his supposed reappearance as an illusion on the part of the disciples, resulting from the intensity of their feelings respecting him. But such an illusion — improbable in any case — could only be possible to minds under the strong excitement of restored faith. This explanation, therefore, leaves still unanswered the question how their faith was restored. How could they, who knew that their Master was dead, and his cause was prostrate, gain faith enough to prompt the strong imagination, not in one mind alone, but in many, that they saw him alive?

The belief of St. Paul that he had seen the Savior, is accounted for by this writer from an excitable nervous temperament, subject to epileptic attacks, and disposed to see visions. This theory does great injustice to one of the most powerful minds that have ever existed; and the difficulty of accounting for the excitement that produced the vision, is increased in his case by the fact, that he was not a mourning friend of Jesus, but a determined enemy of his cause. (Strauss's Life of Jesus, for the German People, Book I. 48, 49.)

INSTITUTIONS OF CHRISTIANITY.

SECTION 11. EVIDENCE FROM INSTITUTIONS.

WE have next to present an argument from the existence of certain institutions connected with our religion. The present bears the impress of the past. We have reasoned, that, as Christianity now exists as the religion of the civilized world, there must have been some adequate cause to produce that prevalence; so we have now to reason from its institutions to the cause that brought them into being. This proof is independent of every other, and would continue, even if the Old and New Testaments were lost. As they exist, however, it confirms their statements.

Institutions preserved among large bodies of men from age to age, afford proof of the reality of those events to commemorate which they were established. We Americans observe the Fourth of July to commemorate the declaration of our national independence. That observance, so long as it is continued, will be a proof that the country was once subject to Great Britain, and that it threw off that subjection. If the whole world should relapse into barbarism, and all historical records should perish, this observance, if it was still kept up, would prove the events on which it was founded. When civilization revived, those who endeavored to restore some knowledge of the past would derive from this institution important testimony. The generation then living would assert that they had received this custom from their fathers, and that these in turn had said that they received it from theirs. If any one should assert that the custom might have sprung up in the dark ages that had intervened, the reply would be, that no nation, however ignorant, could be persuaded to commemorate, as a well-known event in their own history, something which they had never heard of before; still less to believe, and to teach their children, that this new observance was an old custom which they had received from former generations. The keeping of the day, then, must have arisen from some cause well known at the time, and important enough to warrant such a commemoration; and as all the people throughout the country had the same tradition that this cause was the declaration of independence of the British government, there could be no question that such a declaration had taken place.

Apply this to the institutions of the Old Testament. The Passover was the Independence festival of the Jews. (Exodus xii. 3-11; John xii. 1.) It is observed among them still, wherever they are scattered through the world; and they all declare that they observe it to commemorate their deliverance from Egyptian bondage by an especial act of divine power. Profane history testifies that they have thus observed it for at least two thousand years; but, independently of that evidence, the fact of their present observance gives sufficient testimony, not only for that time, but for a much longer period. No one could have persuaded the Hebrews of any generation to adopt a new custom and believe it had been handed down to them by their fathers, in commemoration of a great national deliverance, when no such deliverance had ever taken place.

The observance of the Passover by the Jews thus proves beyond question the event with which it is connected in their tradition — the deliverance from Egypt. It does not, of course, prove the truth of any particular account of that deliverance; but, testifying to the fact itself, it strengthens our faith in the general correctness of the history which records it.

In the same way the Feast of Tabernacles (Lev. xxiii. 34) proves the wandering of the Israelites in the desert; the Feast of Purim (Esther ix. 20–32), still observed among the Jews, proves that there was a historical foundation for the Book of Esther; and the Sabbath, the Ten Commandments (Exodus xx.), the distinction between clean and unclean meats (Levit. xi.), and other Jewish institutions, confirm the truth of those scriptures in which their origin is described.

Still more important to us, as Christians, is the evidence afforded by the institutions peculiar to the New Testament — the Christian ministry and worship, the ordinance of baptism, and especially that of the Lord's Supper. We will exemplify the argument in the last-mentioned instance. In nearly all assemblies for Christian worship it is customary at stated intervals to engage in an especial observance, in which bread and wine are partaken, and certain words repeated as having been spoken by the Founder of the religion: "This is my body, which is given for you;" "This is my blood, of the New Covenant, which is shed for many, for the remission of sins;" "This do in remembrance of me." (Matt. xxvi. 28; Luke xxii. 19.) These words are essentially the same in all churches, and under whatever variety of forms. Let us suppose that this rite did not now exist, and had never been heard of, — would it be possible for any one, however eminent in power or genius, to induce the Christian world to receive it as an institution they had known from childhood, and as having come down from the first age of Christianity? Such a deception would be impossible now, and equally impossible in any former age. The institution, then, must have come down from the first age of Christianity.

Now let us observe the meaning of the words repeated in the observance — words as intimately associated with it as an inscription with the monument on which it is engraved. These words imply, first, that the ordinance was established by the Founder of the religion. They are in the first person singular: "This is *my* body." We have here, then, a memorial from Jesus himself.

They imply, secondly, that this Teacher foresaw his own violent death, and that his anticipation was fulfilled. Had it not been, the observance would have been a mockery.

They imply, thirdly, that he had this foresight, while at liberty and at ease, seated at table with his friends. He could, then, have fled from his enemies. Instead, he employed those precious moments in instituting a rite commemorative of the death he was incurring.

They imply, then, fourthly, his possession of prophetic foresight and unshaken courage, his voluntary endurance of a violent death, the affection for his followers which made him wish to secure their loving remembrance of him, and the confidence in the justice of his cause, which assured him that they would thus remember him.

Lastly, the present existence of this rite shows that these anticipations were fully confirmed; that the cause of Jesus did prevail, notwithstanding his death; and that the reverence and affection of his followers have continued to this day.

This ordinance, then, by itself, presents sufficient proof that the Founder of Christianity endured a voluntary death for the sake of mankind; that he displayed, in its anticipation, unequalled dignity, heroic courage, tender friendship, and prophetic foreknowledge. Could these have been the qualities of a weak enthusiast, or of a wicked deceiver?

EVIDENCE OF THE RECORD.

I. EXTERNAL EVIDENCE.

SECTION 12. THIRD AND FOURTH CENTURIES.

WE have already observed, that, among the religions prevalent in the world, that of the Bible alone claims to rest on historical evidence, proving miraculous authentication.

The life and teachings of Jesus, and the miraculous proofs of his claim to a divine commission, had their date in an age of intelligence and of literary culture; were testified to by those who witnessed them, recorded in part by these, and in part by their immediate followers. The truth of these accounts was maintained by those who gave them, at the peril of their lives. They were received as true by the community of Christians, who had the best means of knowing whether they were true or not; and no accounts contradictory to these were thus received. Some legendary additions were afterwards invented, but they were not admitted by the church as genuine; and they are easily distinguishable from the true accounts, contrasting strongly with them by their indications of weakness, folly, and superstition.

The records of Christianity are the books of the New Testament, and especially the four Gospels and the Acts of the Apostles.

To say that a book is *genuine*, means that it is the

production of the person whose name it bears; to say that it is *authentic*, means that the relations which it gives are correct.

We have reason to believe in the genuineness and authenticity of the New Testament writings, alike from external and internal evidence. We will consider first that which is external — that is, from the testimony given by other writers.

The four Gospels, and the other books of the New Testament, have the same traditional evidence of their genuineness and authenticity on which we receive other productions of a distant age. They have been given to us, as the work of the writers whose names they bear, by those who went before us; they accepted them as such from those who went before them; and so on to the beginning.

The original manuscripts of the Gospels have probably long since perished. Many manuscripts exist, however, and some of great antiquity. About six hundred and seventy Greek manuscripts of the four Gospels, or of different ones among them, have been examined, and some of these bear marks of having been written as early as the fifth century. Besides these, there are numerous manuscripts of early versions of the Gospels, in eleven different languages; and there are others, of the works of the Christian Fathers, or early writers, in which very numerous quotations from the Gospels occur.

It is generally admitted that the Gospels, as we have them now, were in common use at the end of the second century, or the year 200 from the birth of Christ. It is needless, therefore, to say much of the numerous writers who have quoted them since that time. A few, however, may well be mentioned.

The year of our Lord 312 marks the era of the ascendency of Christianity in the Roman empire, which then included all the south of Europe, the north of Africa, and much of the west of Asia. In that year, Constantine, who favored Christianity, defeated his rival Maxentius, and entered Rome in triumph. Early in his reign, Eusebius, bishop of Cæsarea, wrote a history of Christianity, in which he distinctly names our sacred books, attributing them to the same authors to whom they are now ascribed. He speaks, indeed, of a few of the less important, as having had their authorship doubted, but asserts the unquestioned genuineness of the four Gospels, the Acts, thirteen Epistles of Paul, the First of John, and the First of Peter. The discrimination thus made shows that the early Christians did not receive, with blind credulity, every writing that claimed apostolic origin, and thus furnishes a strong proof in favor of those whose claims they unanimously admitted. The date of Eusebius may be fixed in the year 315.

Origen, of Alexandria in Egypt, died in 253. He devoted his learning and industry to the exposition of the books of Scripture, as early as 216. He declares that "the four Gospels alone are received without dispute by the whole church of God under heaven." His quotations are so numerous that it has been said, "If we had all his works remaining, we should have before us almost the whole text of the Bible."

Early in the same century, Tertullian of Carthage gave equally distinct testimony. It has been observed that there are in his writings alone more and larger quotations from the small volume of the New Testament than there are from the numerous works of Cicero in all the writers of several successive ages.

Clement of Alexandria, shortly before Tertullian, gives an account, which he says he had received from presbyters of more ancient times, of the order in which the Gospels were written; and speaks of them as of the highest authority, distinguishing between them and another narrative, then extant, called "the Gospel according to the Egyptians."

An ancient fragment, known as "the Muratorian Canon," is identified as having been written about the year 200, by allusions in it to persons then or recently living. It contains a list of books then received as of canonical authority. In this list are mentioned the four Gospels, the Acts, thirteen Epistles of Paul, two of John, that of Jude, and the Apocalypse. The fragment derives its name from having been discovered, about a century and a half since, in the Ambrosian library at Milan, by the celebrated antiquarian Muratori.

SECTION 13. FIRST AND SECOND CENTURIES.

Among the writers of the second century we select first Irenæus, bishop of the Christian church at Lyons. He was probably born at Smyrna, about A. D. 130, and died about the end of the century. In his youth, at Smyrna, he had been a disciple of Polycarp, who had himself been a hearer of the apostle John. He had thus the best means of information, while his residence in different parts of the empire must have made him familiar with the opinions of Christians both in the east and the west. He expressly relates the origin of the four Gospels. "Matthew," he says, "among the Jews, wrote a Gospel in their own language, while Peter and Paul were preaching the gospel at Rome, and founding a church there. And after their exit, Mark also, the disciple and interpreter of Peter, delivered to us in writing the things that had been preached by Peter; and Luke, the companion of Paul, put down in a book the Gospel preached by him. Afterwards, John, the disciple of the Lord, who also leaned upon his breast, he likewise published a Gospel while he dwelt at Ephesus, in Asia."

Pothinus, the predecessor of Irenæus in the charge of the church at Lyons, was ninety years old about A. D. 170, when that church, with their brethren of Vienne, sent a letter to some eastern churches, giving an account of the sufferings of their martyrs. This letter, which still remains, has exact references to the Gospels of Luke and John, and to the Acts. This indicates that the writers had been taught to hold these books in honor by their instructor, who must have known how they were regarded by Christians in his earlier years.

Justin Martyr was born about A. D. 103, at Neapolis, in Samaria, — anciently Shechem, — and suffered death for his religion at Rome, about A. D. 165. He has, in his two principal writings, between twenty and thirty distinct quotations from the Gospels and the Acts. He recounts almost the entire history of the Savior, agreeing with the scriptural narrative in all but two instances. One of these is a sentence ascribed to our Lord, which appears to be incorrectly quoted; the other, the relation of a circumstance at his baptism, not mentioned by the evangelists, but derived apparently from some other account.

Justin refers to the Gospel of John, not by name indeed, but in three very marked instances; ascribing the term "Logos," or "Word," to the Savior (John i.), quoting the answer of the Baptist to the emissaries from Jerusalem (John i. 20), and that of the Savior to Nicodemus. (John iii. 3.) These quotations are of great importance, as proving the antiquity of this Gospel, which has been especially the object of attack by recent writers. It has been contended, however, on the ground of a slight difference in Justin's language from that of our common copies of John's Gospel, that he did not quote from that, but from some other document, now lost. But the very ancient Greek manuscript lately discovered at Mount Sinai shows that Justin quoted John's Gospel correctly, and thus proves its existence and received authority in the middle of the second century. (See Christian Examiner for May, 1866, article on Tischendorf, by Dr. Hedge.)

The date of Papias is about twenty years before that of Justin, in the earlier part, therefore, of the second century. A fragment of his writing, preserved by Eusebius, tells us that Mark derived his Gospel from the preaching of Peter, and that the Gospel of Matthew was first written in Hebrew. This statement accords with that of Irenæus, already mentioned.

Polycarp, Bishop of Smyrna, respecting whom we have the testimony of his pupil Irenæus, suffered martyrdom in the same persecution with Justin; but, from his great age, his testimony goes farther back. It is stated, that when life was offered him on condition that he would revile Christ, he replied, "Eighty and six years have I served him, and he never did me wrong: how then can

I revile my King and my Savior?" Polycarp had been a scholar of the apostle John; and his pupil Irenæus records that he used to relate his conversations with John and others who had seen the Savior, "both concerning his miracles and his doctrine." An epistle of Polycarp remains, containing nearly forty allusions to books of the New Testament. Among the historical books, his allusions are to passages in Matthew and Luke, and in the Acts.

Clement, bishop or presiding officer of the church in Rome, is referred to by Paul as his "fellow-laborer," in Philippians iv. 3. An epistle of this companion of the earliest teachers still exists, in which he quotes from the Gospel of Matthew, not naming it indeed, but repeating passages of some length. He quotes, in the same manner, from the Epistle to the Romans, the First to the Corinthians, and that to the Hebrews.

The three witnesses we have named last, with some others, are called the "Apostolical Fathers," as having lived in the times of the apostles, and in personal intercourse with them. This is fully established with regard to Polycarp, and appears to us to be so with regard to Clement. For Papias we have the testimony of Irenæus, in the next generation, who calls him a "hearer of John, and companion of Polycarp." He himself quotes as his instructor "John the Elder;" but the language of Irenæus shows that this was no other than John the Evangelist. (See 2 John i.; 3 John i.; 1 Peter v. 1; Eusebius, Hist. Eccl. iii. 39; Rawlinson's Bampton Lectures, p. 465.)

Justin, Polycarp, and Clement of Rome, while giving the testimony which has been described to the facts recorded in the Gospels, do not quote those writings by the names of their authors. Hence, modern ingenuity has imagined that they used other Gospels than those we now possess. On this we remark, —

1. It is admitted that there were, in the first age, other accounts of the life of Jesus. (Luke i. 1.) They probably were imperfect, or by authors little known, and therefore fell into neglect on the appearance of full accounts from the pens of apostles and their companions.

2. If those accounts had differed, as far as they went, from those we now have, they would have been preserved on account of that very difference.

3. The references in these early Fathers agree with our present Gospels, sufficiently establishing that these are the same that they used.

4. Papias distinctly testifies to the authorship of Gospels by Matthew and Mark.

Section 14. Subject continued. Heretical Writers.

The testimony of the ancient Fathers in favor of the historical books of the New Testament, and of the greater part of the Epistles, derives additional force from the fact that there were some books which did not receive from them the same strong attestation. This has been observed already, in regard to Eusebius. Among writers before his time, Dionysius of Alexandria, A. D. 247, expressed doubts concerning the authorship of the book of Revelation. Origen, somewhat earlier, questioned that of the Epistle to the Hebrews, and the Second of Peter; and Caius, about A. D.

200, denied that Paul wrote the Epistle to the Hebrews. These facts prove that the early Christians did not receive without discrimination whatever writing purported to be of apostolic origin, but that they examined carefully, and only yielded their assent where the evidence was satisfactory. Notwithstanding the doubts referred to, the vast majority of Christians since have received as genuine the books which had thus been questioned; how much more reason is there for receiving those more important documents, the Gospels, the Acts, and most of the Epistles, whose claims appear to have been undisputed from the first!

The correctness of the accounts in the Gospels may be strongly inferred from the deep interest which the early Christians took in the life and teachings of their Master. His personal history was the basis of their instruction. Their teachers were constantly preaching "Jesus Christ, and him crucified," "Jesus and the Resurrection." (Acts xvii. 18; 1 Cor. ii. 2.) "Now, there can be no supposition," says Mr. Norton, "more irrational, than that the history of Christ, which was thus promulgated by all his first disciples, and received by all their first converts, was lost before the beginning of the second century, and another history substituted in its place." (Genuineness of the Gospels, vol. iii. p. 312.)

The ancient writers quoted above are from the main body of Christian believers, generally designated as "Catholic," or "Orthodox." But there were others in the first age of Christianity who have been, justly or unjustly, branded as "heretics." An additional proof of the genuineness and authenticity of the New Testament books is afforded by the concurrence of these in their favor.

The earliest among them were the Ebionites, Jewish Christians, who continued to regard their ancient Law as in force, even after the destruction of Jerusalem. They had a Gospel in the Hebrew language; and comparing this fact with the testimony of Irenæus and Papias, we have reason to believe it was the Gospel of Matthew. (See pp. 42, 43.)

Next to these were the Gnostics, a numerous class, including a variety of sects. While the Ebionites were Jews, who retained their Jewish feelings, the Gnostics were converts from heathenism, who retained the habits of thought which had been familiar to their heathen philosophy. They claimed, as their name implies, superior knowledge, and appear to have formed systems of faith for themselves, by combining what pleased them in Christianity with a refined or allegorical mythology. They were inclined to reject whatever was Jewish, maintaining even that the God of the Jews was not the Supreme Being. They would, therefore, have been very unlikely to receive books from Jewish sources, unless coming to them with the strongest attestation of their truth. It is stated, however, by those early writers, from whom we derive our knoweledge of this sect, that Marcion, one of their leaders, A. D. 140, selected from the Gospels that of Luke as the best, and made use of it, omitting the first two or three chapters, for the reason that they were contrary to his views. He did not, it appears, call in question the actions, the miracles, or the apparent sufferings of the Savior; maintaining, however, that these last were only in appearance.

Heracleon, a Gnostic leader, about A. D. 125, is asserted to have written commentaries upon Luke and

John. Valentinus, at the same period, shows an acquaintance with the ideas and style of John's Gospel, and is asserted by Irenæus to have made use of it. The Montanists, another sect of very early date, must have derived from this Gospel their idea of the Paraclete (John xiv. 16, 26); and the Alogi, who objected to the doctrine of the "Logos" (John i.), prove by their very existence the antiquity of the Gospel to which they objected. (See Christian Examiner, article quoted on page 43.)

Basilides, A. D. 120, wrote a commentary, but whether upon all the Gospels, or only on some of them, does not appear. He was certainly acquainted with that of Matthew; and according to the testimony of an ancient work, recently discovered, he quoted also that of John. The work referred to is a treatise on Heresies, ascribed to Hippolytus, bishop of Portus, A. D. 225.

Thus the life of Christ, as we receive it, had the early acknowledgment of the Gnostic sect, notwithstanding the repugnance of their views to anything from a Jewish source. No other work, claiming the title of Gospel, appears to have been in use with them at this early period. The later Gnostics had some books which they called by that name, but they do not appear to have been accounts of the life of Jesus.

It is asserted by Tertullian, A. D. 220, that the Gnostics undertook to prove their doctrines from the New Testament. He objects to their right to do this, on the ground that these Scriptures properly belonged to the regular Christian churches, which could trace the doctrines they held back to the times of the apostles. His argument proves that the churches then existing claimed an uninterrupted connection with the first Christian teachers, who lived not more than a century and a half before; and it proves, too, that the New Testament was acknowledged as authority, both by these churches and their opponents.

"Without enumerating," says Paley, "the later sects of heretics, so called, who, with few and slight exceptions, received the same books as their orthodox brethren, we find that the Sethians, the Montanists, the Marcosians, Hermogenes, Praxeas, and Artemon, all included under that name between the years 150 and 200, received the Scriptures of the New Testament."

SECTION 15. JEWISH AND HEATHEN WRITERS. VERSIONS. COINS.

Various Jewish writers have, at different periods, published works in which testimony was incidentally given with regard to Christianity.

The Talmuds were composed as early as the second century. They speak of Jesus, and of several of his disciples; of his crucifixion; of his miracles, the reality of which they do not question, but represent them as wrought by magical power. They thus add the testimony of their national tradition to the truthfulness of the miraculous accounts in the New Testament.

Josephus held a command among the Jews in their fatal rebellion, about A. D. 70. In one passage, as it stands in his works, respectful mention is made of Jesus; and in another, of James, "the brother of Jesus, who is called Christ." These passages, however, are of uncertain

5

genuineness. The evidence of Josephus is of most value in confirming the representations of Jewish history and ideas, presented to us in the Gospels. Thus, to give a few instances, the account he gives of the cruel and suspicious character of the first Herod, and the atrocities that marked the close of his reign, agrees, in its general features, with that presented in the second chapter of Matthew; his account of Herod Antipas, of Herodias, and of John the Baptist, confirms that of the evangelists. (Matt. xiv.) The sudden death of Herod Agrippa I. agrees, as represented by Josephus, with the account in Acts xii.; and the moderate character of Herod Agrippa II., and the fact that he was intrusted with some authority over the Temple, as Josephus declares, agree with the history given in Acts xxv., xxvi.; Josephus, Antiq. xvii. 6; xviii. 5; xix. 8; xx. 8; Bell. Jud. II. 16.

Among heathen writers, the three great opponents of Christianity were Celsus, Porphyry, and Julian. The last, nephew of Constantine, and known as the Emperor Julian the Apostate, lived at a period so late that his evidence is of minor importance. His allusions and references to the Christian Scriptures are very numerous, and he never questions their genuineness.

Porphyry, about A. D. 275, wrote a work against Christianity, which the mistaken zeal of subsequent ages has destroyed. What it contained we have to learn from the replies of Christian writers. From these it appears that Porphyry referred to the Gospels and Acts as the only acknowledged histories of Christ and his religion.

Still more valuable is the evidence of Celsus, a heathen philosopher, who wrote about A. D. 150. His book, like that of Porphyry, is lost; but much may be learned of its contents from the reply of Origen. He tells us that Celsus used these words: "I could say many things concerning the affairs of Jesus, and those, too, different from those written by the disciples of Jesus; but I purposely omit them." This implies the existence of accounts written "by the disciples;" and it can hardly be believed that if Celsus really possessed any evidence of importance contradictory to theirs, he would have suppressed it.

Elsewhere he accuses the Christians of altering the Gospel, referring in proof to certain readings which were different in different copies. This variation, which implied, probably, no evil intent, but only mistakes of transcribers, shows that copies must have been numerous, and that a considerable space of time must have passed since the original writing.

In another place, the Jew whom Celsus introduces closes an argument with the boast, "These things, then, we have alleged to you out of your own writings, not needing any other weapons."

The particulars to which Celsus refers, by way of objection, are such as are contained in our present Gospels. Such are the genealogies in Matthew and Luke; the precept not to resist evil (Matt. v. 39); the woes denounced by Christ (Matt. xxiii. 13–36.); some of the particulars of his trial and crucifixion; and the difference in the accounts of the resurrection, given by the evangelists. He refers distinctly to statements which we find only in the Gospel of St. John, of the character of Christ as the "Logos," or divine Word, and of the effusion of blood and water from the wound in the Savior's side (John i.; xix. 34), thus proving the reception of that Gospel at the early date at which he wrote. That date was less than a hundred years after the earliest of the Gospels claims to have been written. It is evident, from Celsus, that thus early they were acknowledged by Christians, as they are now, to be the authentic records of the life of the Savior. And as the interval of a hundred years is measured by two lives of no extraordinary length, there is reason to believe that the Christians of that age had good grounds for their confidence in these writings.

Besides the evidence of individual writers, we have, to support the claims of the Christian Scriptures, another testimony of great importance. Versions or translations were made of them at a very early date, the Peshito or ancient Syriac probably in the second century, and many others at periods soon after. These versions confirm the general accuracy of the copies of the New Testament which we possess in the original Greek; and their existence shows the high regard in which those writings were held, from the fact that the labor of translating them was so early undertaken. A similar argument may be derived from the existence of commentaries, paraphrases, and harmonies of the Gospels, by Origen, and others of the ancient Greek Fathers.

In some instances, the minute accuracy of accounts in the book of Acts is proved by ancient coins still in existence. One of these, struck at Cyprus, in the days of the magistrate who succeeded Sergius Paulus (Acts xiii 7), shows that he bore the same title, of Proconsul, which the Christian history assigns to his predecessor. Another, of the city of Philippi, proves that it was, as described in Acts xvi. 12, "a colony," or a place where a body of Roman soldiers had been settled. In the same manner, four peculiar expressions, used in the account of the disturbance at Ephesus (Acts xix.), are shown by ancient coins, as well as by other testimony, to be in accordance with the usage of that city. Its presiding deity was called "the great Goddess Diana;" the city professed itself her worshipper by the peculiar term νεωκόρος. (Verse 35.) One magistrate was known as γραμματεὺς, translated "town clerk" in the same verse; and others were designated as "Asiarchs," or chief of Asia. (Verse 31.) (See Rawlinson's Bampton Lectures, p. 488.)

II. INTERNAL EVIDENCE.

SECTION 16. LANGUAGE; GEOGRAPHICAL ACCURACY, &c.

We have next to consider the Internal Evidence of the genuineness and authenticity of the New Testament, and especially of the Gospels. This evidence comes to us from an examination of their contents.

1. We observe first the language in which they are written. It is that of a peculiar period, and a peculiar class of persons. It is Greek, but not such as we find used by native Greek authors. There are frequent Hebrew idioms in it, showing that the writers were of Jewish origin.

Familiar instances of such idioms may be found in the use of "and" for other conjunctions, and the use of "lo," or "behold," as expletive. (Matt. ii. 1, 9, 13,

19. See 1 Sam. xxiii. 1, 3; 1 Kings xiii. 1.) "Answered" is used redundantly in the expression "answered and said." (Luke ix. 49. See 2 Kings vii. 13.) "Thou sayest" is used as an expression of assent, as it would be in Hebrew, with a particle meaning "thus," or "rightly." (Matt. xxvii. 11. See Exodus x. 29.) The expression, "It is easier for a camel to go through the eye of a needle," is proverbial in the Rabbinical writings; and they employ the expression "new birth" for a change of personal character, for which it is never used in classical Greek. (John iii. 3. See also John iii. 10. See Marsh's Michaelis, chap. iv. sect. 3.)

2. The narratives show, throughout, an intimate acquaintance with the geography, history, government, customs, and modes of thought and feeling in Palestine and the other countries where the scene is laid. It is very difficult for a writer of fiction to be accurate in these respects; but the instances are extremely rare in which there is even a seeming inaccuracy regarding them in the writers of the New Testament.

Take, for an example, the fourth chapter of John. The three provinces, Galilee, Samaria, and Judea, are accurately distinguished. (Verses 3 and 4.) This shows the writer to have been familiar with the country of which he is speaking. Even in our time, when books are multiplied by the press, and geography is studied in every school, how many Americans know what county in England lies between Yorkshire and Northumberland? How many Englishmen know what state lies between Ohio and Illinois? Still farther (verse 5), a city of Samaria is named Sychar — a name sufficiently near to identify it with the ancient Shechem, yet changed as it would probably be by a long lapse of time, aided perhaps by national antipathy, for the word Sychar means "drunkard." (See Isai. xxviii. 1.) Reference is made to "a parcel of ground which Jacob gave to his son Joseph," apparently that spoken of in Gen. xlviii. 22. (Compare, also, Gen. xxxiii. 19; xxxv. 4, 5.) The city is within sight of a mountain, where the Samaritans worshipped. (Verse 20.) The hereditary jealousy between Jews and Samaritans (verse 9) is consistent with narratives and sentiments in 1 Kings xii., 2 Kings xvii., Neh. iv., Ecclus. l. 26, and elsewhere. The separation still continues; a scanty remnant of the Samaritans still worship on Mount Gerizim; at its foot is Shechem, on the road from Judea to Galilee; and the well itself is still pointed out to the traveller.

Rénan, an unbeliever in Christianity as a miraculous revelation, bears witness to the astonishing accuracy of the Gospels in their local details. He says, "I have travelled through the evangelical province in every direction; I have visited Jerusalem, Hebron, and Samaria; scarcely any locality important in the history of Jesus has escaped me. All this history, which, at a distance, seems floating in the clouds of an unreal world, thus assumed a body, a solidity, which astonished me. The striking accord of the texts and the places, the wonderful harmony of the evangelical ideal with the landscape which served as its setting, were to me as a revelation. I had before my eyes a fifth gospel, torn but still legible, and thenceforth, through the narratives of Matthew and Mark, instead of an abstract being, which one would say had never existed, I saw a wonderful human form live and move." (Life of Jesus. Introduction.)

Strauss testifies not less distinctly to the perfect accuracy of the complicated statement given by Luke (iii. 1, 2) respecting the date of John the Baptist's preaching. (Life of Jesus, § 48; first German edition, § 44. Rawlinson's Bampton Lectures, p. 501.)

The agreement of the New Testament writers, with what is known from other authorities of the history, the customs, and the feelings of the age and people described, is not less striking than their geographical accuracy. We have seen already (p. 50) that their accounts of the Herod family agree minutely with what we learn from Josephus. Not one educated Christian in a hundred has a correct knowledge of the complicated relations of that family; but the sacred historians never confuse one member of it with another.

Such facts are of the more importance because the Jewish period of Christianity was so short. The Gospel soon found its most numerous adherents among the Gentiles; and after the Jewish war, A. D. 70, national prejudice was deepened on either side, and the remnant of the Jewish Christian church occupied a separate position, and what was at length regarded as an heretical one. Books from that source would not readily be received among the Gentile Christians, unless from authors possessing the highest claims. The peculiarities of the New Testament show that it was written by Jewish Christians; but no Jewish Christians, after the first age, could have gained acceptance for their books among the Gentile branch of the church. It must, therefore, have been written in the first age.

Section 17. Honesty and Consistency. Differences.

3. There are marks of a purpose to tell simply and honestly the truth. Such is the absence of eulogy, or inflated description, indeed of any description whatever, in relation to the person and demeanor of the Savior, or of his prominent followers. The few exceptions, occurring mostly in the Gospel of John, are slight, and indicate how little of this character is to be found. (See John ii. 24, 25; vii. 46; xiii. 1, 3.)

Such, too, is the narration, without any attempt at concealment or palliation, of incidents unfavorable to the intelligence or characters of the first disciples; their slowness to understand their Master; the earthly nature of their expectations and motives; the betrayal of him by one, the denial by another, the desertion by all. (Matt. xvi. 7, 8; xix. 27; xx. 21, 24; xxvi. 47, 56, 70.)

The narrative of the Savior's trial before the Sanhedrim, and subsequently before Pilate, is given without attempt at exaggeration, and represents the examination, unjust as it was, as marked by no slight degree of deliberation. (Matt. xxvi. 57–68; John xviii. 13–28.)

The mention of the doubts, that existed in some minds with regard to the Savior's claims, would have been suppressed by artful partisans. (See Matt. xxviii. 17; Mark xvi. 13, 14; John vii. 5.)

4. There are marks of the deep impression which the Savior's demeanor and words had produced on the minds of those present.

An illustration of this is afforded in the conduct of the

disciples on some occasions, mentioned incidentally, without any apparent purpose, on the part of the narrator, of exhibiting the greatness of the Savior. (Mark x. 32; Luke ix. 45.)

Words in the language which Jesus spoke are sometimes introduced, when the narrative would have been equally clear and correct if only the Greek translation of them had been given. The reason obviously is, that in the instances referred to, the Syriac words were closely connected with some solemn and striking incident, and were thus deeply impressed on the memory of those who heard them, so that their feelings prompted them to repeat those very words. Such an expression is "Talitha cumi." (Mark v. 41.) Another instance is "Ephphatha." (Mark vii. 34.) This use of language not only shows the faithfulness of the writer, but presents a strong proof of the reality of the miraculous events recorded. (See Furness's Remarks on the Four Gospels, p. 204.)

5. The characters described are consistent, each with himself, even their apparent inconsistencies exhibiting such faults as were the natural accompaniments of their respective excellences. Thus Peter, at one moment, receives high commendation from his Master for his bold declaration of faith in his Messiahship. (Matt. xvi. 16.) Shortly after, the same vehemence of character leads him to incur blame. (Verse 22.) He declares that he never will deny his Lord (xxvi. 33), draws the sword in his defence (John xviii. 10), but shortly after denies him. (Matt. xxvi. 70.) Similar marks of this excitable but unstable character may be found in Matt. xiv. 28, 30; John xiii. 6, 9; xxi. 7, 21.

6. That the Gospels are from the hands of different authors is proved by the difference of the narratives. That of Mark is much the shortest, yet he gives some particulars more fully than either of the other writers. (See Mark v. 41; vii. 34; ix. 23, 24.) Matthew and Luke give different, but not necessarily inconsistent, accounts of wonderful events attending the Savior's birth. Matthew alone gives the Sermon on the Mount at length (chapters v., vi., vii.), of which Luke presents only a sketch. (Luke vi. 17–49.) Yet Luke is in general the fullest in his narration, and we have from him alone the parables of the Good Samaritan (x. 30); of the Prodigal Son (xv. 11), and of the Rich Man and Lazarus (xvi. 19); the incident of the Penitent Thief (xxiii. 40), and the walk to Emmaus. (xxiv. 13.)

The Gospel of John differs from the others still more widely in its narrative, and also in its style of expression and of thought. He relates occurrences which are mentioned by no other evangelist, as the conversation with Nicodemus (chap. iii.), and with the Samaritan woman (chap. iv.), and the raising of Lazarus (chap. xi.); and he omits much which the others relate. The parables of the Savior, as given by the other evangelists, are stories. (See Luke xii. to xvi.) Those given by John are not stories, but comparisons. (See John x. 1–16; xv. 1–9.) The whole style of John's Gospel is more abstract than that of the others. It dwells more upon the personal character and dignity of the Savior (see chap. viii. 12–59, and passages referred to above), and rises to loftier heights of spiritual grandeur than the other Gospels. (See iv. 21–24; xi. 25; xvii.)

But, notwithstanding these differences, the narrative

in all the Gospels is substantially the same; the character of Jesus, and the great facts of his ministry, his betrayal, self-sacrificing death, and resurrection, are the same in all; the parables in Luke, and the comparisons in John, exhibit the same power of imaginative illustration in the great Teacher; and the representations given in all, of God's love and of man's duty, are in perfect agreement.

That there should be differences between the writers, in regard to style of thought and language, is readily accounted for by their different mental constitutions. That there should be differences in the narratives, in points of secondary importance, is only what takes place whenever a series of occurrences is related by different persons. This is well exemplified by Mr. Norton in the fact that no two Roman historians agree fully in the particulars of the assassination of Julius Cæsar.

Section 18. Undesigned Coincidences.

7. Besides the direct agreement in important points, spoken of above, there are numerous coincidences between the accounts, which afford the stronger proof of the faithfulness of the witnesses, from the fact that they are evidently undesigned. As a specimen of this kind, see Luke xxii. 27, where an allusion is made to the Savior's washing the disciples' feet, as recorded by John, chap. xiii. Without this narrative by John, we should not know what the words in Luke meant, "I am among you as he that serveth." On the other hand, John does not tell us the reason of this impressive lesson of humility; this we learn from Luke (xx. 24), "There

was also a strife among them, which should be accounted the greatest."

In other instances, where the accounts apparently contradict each other, we discover, on examination, that it is only because circumstances omitted by one historian are given by another, perhaps supplying what was needed to explain the narrative of the first. For example, Luke tells us that the Jews brought Jesus before Pilate on a charge of claiming the title of king — a charge involving treason against the existing government; that Pilate asked Jesus if he was a king; that he replied in the affirmative; and that Pilate then said, "I find no fault in this man." Upon this narrative alone, the result to which Pilate came is unaccountable; it seems the acquittal of a prisoner whose only words were an avowal of the truth of the charge against him. (Luke xxiii. 1–4.) But we discover from John, that Pilate in the mean time had examined Jesus in private, and learned from him of the spiritual and unworldly nature of the kingdom he claimed. (John xviii. 33–38.) On the other hand, John gives us no explanation of the reason why Pilate asked the prisoner if he was a king. This Luke supplies, by stating that he was accused of claiming that title. Thus the two narratives, instead of contradicting, fit into and explain each other.

The coincidences among the first three Gospels are very numerous, whole narratives being frequently given in almost the same words. (Compare Matt. ix. 14–17, Mark ii. 18–22, and Luke v. 33–38.) For this reason, some modern writers have practically reduced the number of historians who record the life of Jesus from four to two, maintaining that the first three evangelists, whom they class together under the name of Synoptics, were in effect but different copyists from an original document now lost, or different collectors of the same series of traditional accounts. We reply to this, first, that if an original document had existed, so well known and so highly prized that three of the four Gospels were drawn from it, it would have been carefully preserved, and we should find references to it in the Gospels themselves, and in other early Christian writings; whereas, not only is it not in existence, but not a trace of it remains in ancient record or tradition. That it ever existed at all is but a modern inference.

Secondly, the supposition that the first three evangelists found their materials in the same series of traditional accounts is probably true, with the exception that the accounts were contemporaneous instead of being traditional. Everything relating to the Savior being eagerly heard and constantly repeated, there must have been, current in the primitive churches, an unwritten life of Christ, expressed in words which the sacred historians naturally adopted, except where their separate information gave them reason for departing from it. (See Norton's Genuineness of the Gospels, vol. i., note D.)

8. The accounts in the historical books are confirmed by the agreement of the Epistles with them. The most important of these are of unquestionable genuineness, being admitted even by writers who dispute the authority of the Gospels. (See the quotation from Strauss, p. 30.) They have been received as genuine from the first age, and from the nature of the case, forgery would have been nearly impossible without detection; for they are evidently portions of a correspondence; letters some-

times referring to former letters (2 Cor. vii. 8; 2 Thess. ii. 2); at other times discussing questions then agitating the church (1 Cor. viii. 1; x. 25); elsewhere dealing with personal matters, and containing personal salutations. (Rom. xvi; Philemon.) The accounts they give of Christianity agree, in all important respects, with those of the Gospels and the Acts.

As instances of this coincidence, we may notice, first, that the resurrection of the Savior is described by all the four Evangelists, and is represented in the Acts as occupying a place of the highest importance in the preaching of the apostles. (Acts xvii. 18.) Compare with this the expressions on the same subject in the Epistles. (1 Cor. xv. 12–18; Col. ii. 12; 1 Thess. i. 10; 2 Tim. ii. 8.)

The account of the institution of the Lord's Supper, given in the Gospels, is confirmed in 1 Cor. xi. 23–26.

The peculiar character of the apostle Peter, ardent, but subject to sudden changes of purpose, already commented on as displayed in the Gospels (see p. 58), is exhibited alike in an incident narrated in Gal. ii. 11–14.

Section 19. Agreement of Luke's Writings with the Epistles.

The agreement between different portions of the New Testament is most strikingly observable with regard to the Gospel of Luke and the Acts, when taken in connection with the Epistles. These various writings are connected together, and their authenticity established, by a peculiar chain of internal evidence. For distinctness' sake we will designate the links of this chain by Roman numerals.

I. There are very numerous coincidences between the Acts and the Epistles, which establish the authority of the Acts as a history, and that of the Epistles as genuine letters of the apostle. This evidence has been brought forward in a very convincing manner in the Horæ Paulinæ of Dr. Paley. To exemplify it, we select the following instances: —

In Gal. i. 18, the apostle speaks of visiting Jerusalem the first time after his conversion, and remaining only fifteen days. So short a stay in that city, on a visit which must have been alike interesting and important to himself and to the Christians there, seems to require explanation. We find this in Acts ix. 29, and again in Acts xxii. 18, from which we learn that he left hastily, in consequence of designs against him.

From 1 Thess. iii. 1, 2, 6, it appears that Paul was for a time alone at Athens, having sent Timothy to Thessalonica, and that Timothy joined him afterwards. The history (Acts xvii. 14, 15) agrees with this, except that Timothy is left at Berea, instead of being sent to Thessalonica. This difference shows that the history and the Epistle were not artfully conformed to each other. In fact there is no real disagreement; but only the historian, writing briefly, omitted to mention the sending of Timothy to Thessalonica, thus leaving the cause of his absence from Paul unexplained.

It is implied in 1 Cor. i. 12, and iii. 6, that Apollos preached at Corinth after Paul had left that city. This agrees with what is incidentally expressed in the history. (Acts xviii. 1, 24–28; xix. 1.)

We learn from Rom. xv., that Paul, at a late period of his ministry (see verse 19), intended to go to Jerusalem (verse 25), to carry to the Christians there a collection made for them by those in Macedonia and Achaia (verses 26, 28), but that he anticipated danger from the opponents of Christianity at Jerusalem. (Verse 31.) The account in Acts agrees with this in every particular. Paul, at a late period of his ministry (chap. xx.), returned from Achaia, or Greece (verse 2), through Macedonia (verse 3), to Syria. He was on his way to Jerusalem (verse 22), with anticipations of danger (verses 22, 23), and on an errand of charity (xxiv. 17); and his anticipations of danger were fulfilled.

The above are but a few specimens of the very numerous coincidences, often in minute particulars, and obviously undesigned, which prove alike the genuineness of the Epistles and the knowledge and faithfulness of the historian.

II. The fact that this historian was a companion of the apostle Paul, which might be inferred from the fulness and accuracy of his accounts, is established by the manner in which he uses the pronoun *we* when describing the journeys of the apostle. (Acts xvi. 10, 11, 16; xx. 13, 14; xxvii., xxviii.)

III. The abrupt manner in which the book of Acts terminates shows that it was written during the life of Paul, and when he had been about two years a prisoner at Rome. (Acts xxviii. 30, 31.)

IV. The Gospel of Luke and the Acts were written by the same person. This is proved by the prefaces or introductions to both. (Luke i. 1–4; Acts i. 1.)

V. The Gospel of Luke was written before the Acts; that is, as early at least as the second year of Paul's imprisonment in Rome, or A. D. 62. (Acts i. 1.)

Thus the Epistles and Acts sustain each other, and the Acts sustains the Gospel; all proving that this account of the Savior's life was written by a companion of the apostle Paul, not more than about thirty years after the crucifixion.

Section 20. Writings of the Apostle John.

A train of argument somewhat similar furnishes proof of the genuineness and authenticity of the writings ascribed to the apostle John.

I. The writer of the Gospel claims for himself (or, if the passage, John xxi. 24, is from another hand, then some witness, very near the time of writing, claims for him) that he was one of the apostles, and distinguished by the especial love of his Master.

II. The style of this writer is marked by peculiar expressions, which occur alike in the Gospel and the Epistles, and one of them in a remarkable passage in the Revelation. (Compare John i. 1–4 with 1 John i. 1, 2, and Rev. xix. 13. Also John xiii. 34, and 2 John, 5; John xxi. 24, and 3 John 12.)

III. If these works were from the same pen, and the writer an apostle, we learn from Rev. i. 1, 4, 9, that he was the apostle John.

IV. The comment on a supposed prediction of the Savior, in John xxi. 23, indicates that the disciple to whom it applied was yet living, and appears to be from his own pen.

V. The designation of one of the apostles by the terms "another disciple" (xviii. 15), and "the disciple whom Jesus loved" (xxi. 20), seems only to be accounted for by the fact that he was himself the writer. It is hard to conceive the motive which any other person would have to suppress the name.

VI. There is a prominence given to this apostle, in several occurrences, omitted or less minutely narrated in the other Gospels, and in some of which he appears in marked superiority to Peter. (See John xiii. 23; xviii. 15, 16; xix. 26; xx. 4, 8; xxi. 7, 20–22.) It is difficult to account for this without admitting that this apostle was the author of the Gospel. Rénan conjectures that a degree of vanity or self-interest influenced his judgment or his recollection. (Life of Jesus, Wilbour's translation, pp. 26, 27, 322, 349.) This would naturally exhibit itself, not in false statements, but in the selection of incidents that were most favorable to himself. This supposition, therefore, while it presents the apostle as liable to human imperfection, does not seriously affect his credibility as an historian. More probably these were instances of faithful simplicity of narration, the facts being known to the writer more fully because he was an actor in them; but he was himself aware how difficult it would be to write the life of his Master and Friend without making himself prominent, and therefore with studious modesty veiled his own name under circumlocutions. Another theory to account for his prominence in this Gospel is, that it was written, not by John himself, but by his attached disciples, from their remembrance of what he had told them. If so, the Gospel is still, in substance, his testimony. But this theory is less probable, as his disciples, intent on doing him honor, would have made his name conspicuous, instead of concealing it.

Among the arguments which have been urged, especially by writers of what is called "the Tübingen school," against the genuineness of John's Gospel, the most important are, the different representation which it gives of the scene and manner of the Savior's instructions; its peculiar language concerning the Logos, the Word, or personified Wisdom of God; the remarkable character of its leading miracle, — that of the raising of Lazarus,— which, it is said, could not have been omitted by the other evangelists if it had actually taken place; and a difference between the account of this Gospel and that of the others with regard to the date of the last supper, and consequently of the crucifixion. The others represent the last supper as identical with the feast of the passover. (Matt. xxvi. 19; Mark xiv. 16; Luke xxii. 13.) John appears to place it before that feast. (John xiii. 1; xviii. 28.)

In answer to these arguments we have first to observe, that the difference between the accounts of John and those of the other writers is owing in part to the different style of that apostle, and in part to an obvious purpose not to repeat what had been said before. His Gospel appears to be supplementary to the others; and this, not only in the facts it records, but in its doctrine. The personal attachment of the writer to his Lord led him to record, more fully than the three preceding writers, those discourses in which Jesus asserted his own dignity (chapters v., vi., x.); and his spiritual insight made him appreciate and remember such instructions as those respecting the new birth, and the promise of the Comforter. (Chap. iii., xiv. 16, 26.)

The exalted and mysterious dignity of the Savior, however, is expressed in Matt. xi. 27 as strongly as in almost any passage in John; and we find promises of the assistance of the Holy Spirit in such passages as Matt. x. 19, 20; Luke xxiv. 49.

It is urged by the writers in question, that the language of this Gospel with regard to the "Word" (in Greek, Logos, John i. 1–14) resembles that in use among those who, under the name of Gnostics, endeavored to combine Christianity with some heathen views which claimed the name of philosophy. Hence they infer that this Gospel was not written until such views had become diffused, fixing its date at about A. D. 150. In reply to this, we may remark, that the doctrine concerning the Logos, the personified Wisdom of God, appears in the writings of Philo, a learned Jew of Alexandria, who was contemporary with the Savior, and whose works had probably found admirers in those populous and cultivated cities of Asia Minor where John ministered. Besides, the title, "The Word of God," is applied to Christ, with high attributes of majesty, in the Apocalypse, which the Tübingen critics recognize as the genuine work of this apostle.

The omission by the other evangelists of the narrative respecting Lazarus, has been accounted for by the supposition that he was yet alive when the earlier evangelists wrote, and that they feared to bring upon him that persecution of which he had already been in danger. (John xii. 10.) We would suggest another explanation — that none of the disciples but John accompanied the Savior to Bethany, he having sent the others before to Jerusalem, while he remained with his chosen friend to visit the afflicted family.

The apparent difference with regard to the Last Supper is explained by the supposition that John used the term "Passover," in reference not merely to the observance of the first day, but to that of the whole festival season. (Lev. xxiii. 5, 6.)

Whatever strength there may be in the arguments alleged, it cannot, in our opinion, compare with that derived from the spiritual character of this Gospel. If it is not authentic, the "moral miracle" of Christianity (see p. 25) is doubled. We have, then, not only to account for the wonderful Teacher who gave the Sermon on the Mount and the Parables, but for another mind, of genius and tenderness equal to his, who invented the conversation with Nicodemus (John iii.), that with the Samaritan woman (iv.), the raising of Lazarus (xi.), and the parting conversation with the disciples. (xiii.–xvii.) And this man, of glorious intellect and feeling heart, has left no remembrance of his name, no trace of his existence, except this forgery, in which he endeavors to palm off his own thoughts and words as those of Jesus! Well may Rénan make the admission, "We have no example, in the apostolic world, of a forgery of this kind." (Life of Jesus, p. 26.)

Section 21. Apocrypha of the New Testament.

The endeavor has sometimes been made to depreciate the authentic Gospels, by representing them as of the same class with certain other writings, which are known as the "Apocrypha of the New Testament." These works have come down to us from an early period of Christian history, mostly in the Greek, but partly in the Arabic language. Collections of them, in the original languages, with Latin translations, have been published in Germany; and they have also been translated into English. It will appear, we trust, on examination, that these writings, instead of diminishing, should confirm our confidence in the records of the Christian faith.

We do not deny that there were other attempts, in the primitive age, to write the history of the Savior, besides those which resulted in our present Gospels. This we infer from the preface of Luke. (i. 1.) These accounts, however honestly designed, were probably from imperfect information, or unskilfully put together, so that they fell into disuse after the publication of the authentic Gospels. The most important of them was the Gospel according to the Hebrews, if indeed this was not, as there is some reason for believing, the Hebrew original of Matthew's Gospel. This is quoted once by Clement of Alexandria, and twice by Origen. A Gospel according to the Egyptians is also mentioned; but Clement of Alexandria, who refers to it, says that he had never seen it; yet his residence in Egypt, and his zeal as a scholar, would have made him acquainted with it if it had been considered of much value or authority. Neither of these books is included, or claimed to be included, in the collections mentioned above; nor is either of them, as far as is known to scholars, now in existence. These exceptions, if they can be considered such, hardly invalidate the assertion of Paley, "that, besides our Gospels and the Acts of the Apostles, no Christian history, claiming to be written by an apostle or apostolical man, is quoted within three hundred years after the birth of Christ, by any writer now extant or known; or, if quoted, is not quoted without marks of censure or rejection." (Evidences of Christianity, Prop. I., chap. ix., sect. 11.)

The writings called the "Apocrypha of the New Testament" are productions of various ages. But the earlier they are dated, the more obvious appears the contrast between their contents and those of the authentic Gospels. The character of the narratives may be fairly estimated from the following specimens: —

"The following accounts we find in the book of Joseph the high priest, called by some Caiaphas. He relates that Jesus spoke even when he was in his cradle, and said to his mother, Mary, 'I am Jesus, the Son of God, the Word, which thou didst bring forth according to the declaration of the angel Gabriel to thee; and my Father hath sent me for the salvation of the world.'" (First Infancy, chap. i. verse 1.)

A boy possessed with devils is cured by the touch of the swaddling clothes of Jesus. "The devils began to come out of his mouth, and fly away in the shape of crows and serpents." (First Infancy, iv. 15. Chap. xi. of Thilo's edition, Arabic and Latin.)

The Virgin Mary cures leprosy and other diseases with the water in which the child had been washed. (Chap. vi. and elsewhere.) A young man, who had been changed into a mule, is restored to his proper form by the child being placed upon his back. (Chap. vii.)

Joseph, being employed to make a throne for Herod, makes it too narrow. Jesus, however, directs him to take hold of it on the one side, while himself drawing it on the other, and it is expanded to the proper size. (Chap. xvi.)

Another time, Jesus went forth into the street, and a boy running by rushed upon his shoulder; at which Jesus, being angry, said to him, "Thou shalt go no farther;" and he instantly fell down dead. The parents complain to Joseph, and say, "Either teach him that he bless, and not curse, or else depart hence with him, for he kills our children." Joseph reproves Jesus, who inflicts blindness on the parents who had complained of him. (Second Infancy, or Gospel of Thomas, chap. ii. Thilo's edition, iv. and v. of the Greek.)

In the "Gospel of Nicodemus, or Acts of Pontius Pilate," Carinus and Leucius, sons of Simeon, rise from the dead, and describe to the Council of the Jews the transactions in the world of spirits on occasion of the death of Christ, after which they vanish. Their account is told to Pilate, who, Gentile as he is, is represented as entering into the holy place of the Temple. The high priests identify Jesus as the Messiah, by a prophecy "in the first book of the Seventy, where Michael, the archangel, in speaking to the third son of Adam, the first man, foretells that after five thousand five hundred years, Christ, the most beloved Son of God, was to come on earth." (Thilo, ch. xxviii.) Pilate gives an account of these occurrences to the Emperor Tiberius, who tries him at Rome for crucifying Christ, and condemns him to be beheaded; but Pilate being penitent, his head is received by an angel. (Thilo, pp. 813–816.)

The absurdity of some of these stories, the inconsistency of others with the just and loving character of Jesus, and the contradiction presented by the last to well-known facts connected with the Old Testament, with Jewish customs, and with the early history of Christianity, place these narratives in strong contrast to the genuine Gospels. They show us what those Gospels would have been had they been formed by the imagination of the writers, instead of deriving their accounts from the statements of eye-witnesses. As to their origin, they appear to have been designed to meet from fancy the desires which many felt of knowing more respecting the early years of Jesus, of beholding his cause triumphantly vindicated before Jew and Gentile, and of possessing something in writing from his own hand. This last want is met by a letter purporting to be from Jesus to Abgarus, king of Edessa, who had invited the Savior to reside with him. These writings were not probably composed with the definite intention of deceiving. The Gospel of Nicodemus, especially, may be regarded as a romance of sacred history, and, as such, of some literary merit.

The apocryphal Christian writings which now exist, and those which are lost, so far as anything is known of them, do not contradict, in any important particular, the accounts given in the authentic Gospels. Where they differ, it is by adding to the statements of the evangelists, not by giving narratives opposed to theirs, — that indirect opposition excepted, which results, as in the cases given above, from the writers' neglect of historic truth, or their inability to understand the gentle and merciful character of Jesus.

SECTION 22. RESULT OF OUR INQUIRIES RESPECTING THE RECORD.

It is, then, established by sufficient evidence, that the four Gospels were generally received among Christians as correct histories of their Master, from the earliest age, and that no history inconsistent with theirs was thus received. A similar conclusion may be held with regard to the other books of chief importance in the New Testament, if not to all.

This would be sufficient to entitle these books to be received as the basis of our Christian faith, even if we were ignorant of the names of their authors. For instance, if we are sure that the fourth Gospel contains a true account, it is of little importance to us whether it was written by the apostle John, by some of his disciples, or by others.

We have also, however, proofs of great strength, that these books were the work of the very persons whose names they bear. (See especially the testimony of Irenæus, p. 42; the argument from the connection of the Gospel of Luke with the Acts and the Epistles, p. 64; and that in relation to the Gospel of John, p. 66.)

In further evidence of this, we may observe, —

1. That, having traced these writings back to the apostolic age, there is no reason why we should not believe the general voice of antiquity, which assigns them to certain persons then living, and most likely to be qualified for the task.

2. That this testimony of antiquity is without exception as far as regards the Gospels and the other books

of chief importance. We never find manuscripts of the Gospel of Matthew bearing the name of Luke, nor of Luke bearing that of Peter. No ancient writer asserts that the Gospel which now bears the name of John was written by any other than that apostle. If either of the four Gospels is wrongly assigned, it is strange that not the slightest trace should remain of its true author.

The number of the witnesses is a point of great importance. If we had received the account of the life of Jesus from one alone, there might be a suspicion of fraud or delusion; but it comes to us directly from *four* evangelists, and is confirmed to us by the agreement, expressed or implied, of the other writers of the New Testament. That there should be a combination among so many to deceive, without some one betraying the secret, is highly improbable.

It may be urged as an objection to the trustworthiness of the Christian records, that the ancient manuscripts, versions, and quotations by the Fathers do not always agree together. There are various readings; and these, it is admitted, are numbered by thousands. But it is to be remembered, that nearly all of these are of very slight importance. They arose of necessity in ages when the only way of multiplying copies of books was with the pen. Among them all there are very few that possess any doctrinal importance, and none that disturb at all the great facts of the Christian revelation.

Are these records, then, worthy of our reliance?

They are, if any human testimony can be. Suppose that we had four memoirs of the campaigns of Washington, two by officers in command under him, and the other two by persons in immediate communication with such officers; what more authentic account of those campaigns could we desire?

It is safe to conclude that no objection would be made to the reception of the accounts these books contain, by any person acquainted with the evidence which supports them, but for the miraculous character of their statements. But many modern writers, assuming that miracles are impossible, refuse their assent to the narratives of the Gospels, in whole or in part, on that account.

This is the position of those who in our own age have endeavored to remove the miraculous element from the Christian history. It is a position to which they have been led by the philosophical tendencies of the age, both as connected with the study of outward nature and with metaphysical investigation.

The researches of physical science have given to those familiar with them a deep conviction of the stability of the laws of nature. The common idea of a miracle, therefore, as an event in which all laws of nature are set aside, has been considered inadmissible; and it has not always been sufficiently kept in mind that there may be other and higher laws of nature than those with which we are familiar. (See Section 2.)

In metaphysical philosophy, the German mind has, for a century past, been more active than that of any other nation. In Germany, a system of philosophy has prevailed, known as the Transcendental, and illustrated by the great names of Kant, Fichte, and many others. Of this system it may be sufficient to point out one distinguishing trait — that it looks for proof of truth within, and not without; to the soul of man, not to the external world. Few will deny the nobleness of the direction thus given to investigation; few perhaps will deny that the defenders of Christianity had hitherto been too limited in their efforts — laboring to prove, almost exclusively by outward testimony, that which bore the stamp of heaven in its intrinsic excellence. But the transition is easy from one extreme to its opposite; and the scholars of Germany, in their homage to the light within, were tempted to turn with disgust from the idea of external proof, of miracle, and even of revelation.

From these causes, many recent writers, instead of examining whether the miracles are proved, declare or assume, at the outset, that they are incapable of proof. This fact is of importance to observe, for it shows that their theories are not the conclusions of unbiassed minds, from fair and thorough investigation of the record, but ingenious attempts to turn the Gospel accounts from their obvious meaning, or to undermine their authority, in favor of a preconceived idea. Thus, Strauss says, "No just perception of the true nature of history is possible without a perception of the inviolability of the chain of finite causes, and of the impossibility of miracles." (Life of Jesus, § 13, vol. i. p. 64, English translation.) Rénan protests against the charge of "mutilating the facts in the name of theory;" but he still reaches the conclusion, previous to the examination of the New Testament miracles, "that a supernatural narration cannot be accepted as such." (pp. 43, 45.)

MODERN SPECULATIONS.

SECTION 23. THEORIES THAT SUPPOSE THE GOSPEL NARRATIVES CORRECT.

WE will now present a brief view of the principal classes of attempts that have been made to account for, or to remove, the miraculous element in Christianity.

We have first to name those theories that proceed on the supposition that the Gospel narratives are substantially correct. Among these we must class an explanation of the miracles which admits them to have taken place as narrated, and receives the testimony they bear to the holiness of Jesus, but seeks to ascertain a law of nature in conformity to which they took place. Such has been the effort of Dr. Furness, in his "Remarks on the Four Gospels," and subsequent works, ascribing many of these wonders to the natural influence of a most holy and majestic being over the minds of those whom he addressed, and, through their minds, over their bodily organs. He carries this view so far as to conceive that it will explain even the raising of Lazarus, the commanding voice of Jesus being heard in the spirit world. (Remarks, p. 179, 180.) There are, however, well-attested miracles, to which this theory is obviously inapplicable (see Matt. viii. 27; xiv. 25; xxi. 19; John ii. 9); and even where it is applied, the effect asserted transcends, not only in degree, but in kind, the natural influence of one mind over another in any case within human experience. "Since the world began was it not heard that any man," by the natural power of a virtuous character and a strong faith, "opened the eyes of one that was born blind," much less raised the dead to life. (John ix. 32.) Our dissent from this theory does not prevent us from doing justice to the distinguished ability, and the reverent and loving spirit, in which it has been advocated.

Some German writers, known as the "Naturalists," of whom Professor Paulus is the best known, admitting the literal truth of the accounts given by the Evangelists, represent those accounts as describing events in which there was nothing supernatural. To show the character of their explanations a few examples will be sufficient.

In Matt. xvii. 27, Jesus directs Peter, "Go thou to the sea, and cast a hook, and take up the fish that first cometh up; and when thou hast opened his mouth, thou shalt find a piece of money." According to Paulus, the only purpose of opening the fish's mouth was to take out the hook; and the money was "found" by selling the fish. (Paulus, Life of Jesus, § 136.)

The raising of Lazarus is thus explained: Jesus, from his knowledge of diseases, is convinced that Lazarus could not have really died. He therefore goes to the tomb, and causes the stone to be removed; then, looking into the tomb, he perceives that his impression is correct, for the supposed corpse begins to move. He calls out, therefore, "Lazarus, come forth!" And the accidental resuscitation of Lazarus has the appearance of being the result of that command. (§ 151.)

In explanation of the ascension of Jesus, as described Acts i. 9–11, we are told that Jesus, in taking leave of his disciples, removed himself farther from them. Hereupon, a cloud or mist interposed itself between them, and concealed Jesus from their sight — a result which, on the assurance of two unknown men, they regarded as a reception of Jesus into heaven. (§ 215.)

"In the supposition that the two individuals clothed in white apparel were real men, Paulus only disguises a final and strongly-marked essay of the opinion espoused by Bahrdt and Venturini, that several epochs in the life of Jesus, especially after his crucifixion, were brought about by the agency of secret colleagues. Shall we, with Bahrdt, dream of an Essene lodge into which he retired after the completion of his work? and with Brennecke appeal, in proof that Jesus long continued silently to work for the welfare of mankind, to his appearance for the purpose of the conversion of Paul? Or shall we, with Paulus, suppose that shortly after the last interview, the body of Jesus sank beneath the injuries it had received?" From such modes of representation, "a sound judgment must turn away with aversion." (Strauss, Life of Jesus, iii., v., § 142; first German edition, § 138.)

It is only necessary to add to the condemnation so justly passed by Strauss on the conjectures of his predecessors, that if Jesus claimed to have raised Lazarus from the dead, when the occurrence was only a fortunate accident, or if he deceived his disciples by the aid of unknown confederates, his conduct was that of a hypocritical juggler, utterly inconsistent, therefore, with the principles he proclaimed, and with that intellectual and moral power which has left so deep an impression on the history of the world.

Section 24. Theories supposing Fraud.

Suppositions have been advanced by some writers, more distinctly admitting the idea of fraud, either on the part of Jesus himself or on that of others.

Rénan conceives the character of wonder-worker to have been forced on Jesus by the credulity of those around, rather than willingly assumed (Life of Jesus, pp. 235–239) ; thus excusing his deception at the expense of his firmness and good sense. In one remarkable instance, however, he considers Jesus to have been himself deceived. The raising of Lazarus is supposed to have been a scene, arranged between Lazarus and his sisters, to delude not only the people, but Jesus himself, with the idea that a miracle was performed; and this impious fraud is represented as wrought from enthusiastic love towards the Master upon whom it was practised. (p. 305.)

It is, however, with regard to the resurrection of the Savior that the boldest and most ingenious speculations have been employed. It was indeed necessary to the opponents of miracle, that, if possible, some natural explanation should be found for this great event; for, as we have seen already (section 10), it is sustained by the most ample evidence, and is in fact implied in the very existence of the Christian church. Two ways were suggested to account for it. "The cultivated intellect of the present day," says Strauss, "has very decidedly stated the following dilemma: either Jesus was not really dead, or he did not really rise again. Rationalism has principally given its adherence to the former opinion."

The death of Jesus, consequently, is explained by many writers as having been merely apparent — a swoon or catalepsy, from which he recovered, and appeared before the disciples as if risen from the dead. In support of this opinion, the fact is urged, that cases have been known in which crucifixion did not produce death; and reference has been made to an instance mentioned by Josephus, and to tortures voluntarily endured by certain fanatics in France. In all these cases, however, the victims were taken from the cross for the purpose of saving them, and restorative means applied; so that they would furnish no ground to infer the restoration of Jesus, unless we admit the use of similar means in his case. By whom, then, were these means applied? And on whom is the deception of the world through so many ages to be charged?

The supposition of Bahrdt is, that "Jesus, seeing no other way of purifying the prevalent Messianic idea from the admixture of material and political hopes, exposed himself to crucifixion, but, in so doing, relied on the possibility of a speedy removal from the cross by early bowing his head, and of being afterwards restored by the medical skill of some among his secret colleagues," — those imagined Essene confederates referred to in a previous extract (p. 81), — "so as to inspirit the people at the same time by the appearance of a resurrection." "Others have ascribed to his disciples a preconceived plan of producing apparent death by means of a potion." (Strauss, Part III., chap. iv. § 140.) Such was the theory of Schuster, who conceived also that the awaking of Jesus was aided, and the stone removed from the mouth of the tomb, by an earthquake and lightning, which fortunately occurred at the moment they were needed. (See Strauss, as above.)

Surpassing even these theories in extravagance, if that be possible, is the suggestion of a writer in the Westminster Review (for Jan., 1858), that the person by whom the crucifixion was prevented from being fatal was Pilate himself! That magistrate, it is said, had shown an earnest desire to save the life of Jesus; and when he finally yielded to the importunity of the Jews, he resolved to do secretly what he dared not do openly. He gave private orders, therefore, that the legs of Jesus should not be broken, and that the body should be taken from the cross before life was extinct. It is not explained how one of Pilate's soldiers dared to thrust a spear into the side of the prisoner whom his master meant to save; nor how that thrust, which entered the pericardium, as appeared from the effusion of water with the blood, failed to produce death. (See John xix. 34, 35, and commentators on the passage.)

On these strange fancies, we may briefly remark, that the slow recovery which alone would be possible from natural causes, after the lingering torture had almost extinguished life, is not consistent with the accounts given of the Savior's appearance to the women, and to his disciples, and in particular with the circumstances of the walk to Emmaus. (See Luke xxiv. 13–43; John xx. 14–17, 19.)

We must believe too, upon these suppositions, either that Jesus thought he had been really dead when he had not, which is inconsistent with the wisdom which he always showed, or that he was guilty of an atrocious fraud upon his followers, which is inconsistent alike with his instructions and his example. (See Mark xvi. 14; Luke xxiv. 26, 46; John xx. 27, 29.)

Rénan, taking the other alternative of the dilemma, believes that Jesus actually died on the cross, and ascribes the story of his resurrection principally to "the strong imagination of Mary Magdalene." As two of the Gospels state that her report of the resurrection was at first not credited, and as all agree in mentioning other appearances of the Savior, besides the testimony of Paul to the same effect, we cannot acquiesce in this summary reduction of the number of witnesses. (See Mark xvi. 11, Luke xxiv. 11, and the accounts of the resurrection generally; also 1 Cor. xv. 5–8.)

SECTION 25. THE MYTHICAL THEORY.

Many probably content themselves with distinguishing between the natural and the supernatural narratives in the Gospels; receiving the former and rejecting the latter, simply on the ground that the former are credible and the latter incredible.

But this position cannot consistently be held, since both descriptions of narratives rest on the same testimony. If that testimony is sufficient, we must receive the miracles; if the miracles are pronounced false, the testimony of those who record them is discredited, even when they relate events that were not miraculous. If John was competent to testify to the conversation of Jesus with the sisters of Lazarus, which he heard, he was competent to testify to the raising of Lazarus, which he saw.

Again, in the Gospels, the miraculous and the spiritual or didactic are often interwoven in such a manner that they cannot properly be separated. For instance, in the narrative just referred to, if we suppose the Savior only to have instructed Martha that her brother should rise again (John xi. 23), and to have declared, "I am the resurrection and the life," without the miracle, we leave the account unfinished, and several sentences of it unexplained. (See verses 6, 11, 23–26, 41, 42.) The touching incidents and instructions after the resurrection are evident fictions, unless the resurrection had taken place. (See Luke xxiv.; John xx., xxi.)

The explanation of Dr. D. F. Strauss, known as the Mythical Theory, was not, however, original with him. It had been applied, by many before his time, to portions alike of the Old Testament and of the New. But by him it was developed into a system, and extended, with cold, unsparing sagacity, to every leading incident in the life of Christ. The idea it expresses is, that the stories respecting Jesus arose without intentional deception on the part of any one, partly from exaggerations of actual occurrences, and partly from supposing things to have really taken place which seemed appropriate to his character, either from the declarations of the prophets, the popular expectation among the Jews, or any other cause. These myths or stories Strauss supposes to have been collected by the Evangelists in good faith, and published by them with the belief that they contained the real history of Jesus. But all that is miraculous being set aside as impossible, and events not miraculous being regarded as mythical, wherever any plausible motive could be assigned for their fabrication, there remains little that can be identified as undoubtedly belonging to Jesus.

With regard to this theory, we may observe, —

1. That it is inconsistent with the evidence presented above; proving that the Gospels were written by their reputed authors, who were well qualified to declare the truth respecting the history of Jesus.

2. Fabulous stories are the growth of a very different period from that in which Jesus lived. They arise in the ages of dim tradition, preceding the researches of the historian; but the period of the Savior was an age of intelligence, and of literary cultivation.

3. Fabulous stories, under the most favorable circumstances, are of slow growth. The period allowed by Strauss in his original work, of about thirty years, is altogether too short for their production, and even the longer time allowed in his recent volume appears inadequate.

4. If the supposed myths were founded on Jewish expectations of the Messiah, they would have invested Jesus with some form of temporal royalty. On the contrary, we see him constantly refusing such distinction. (Luke xii. 14; John vi. 15; xviii. 36.)

5. The childish stories of the "Gospels of the Infancy," and the unhistorical acknowledgment of Jesus by Jews and Romans in the "Gospel of Nicodemus," show us what our Gospels would have been had they been written as Strauss imagines.

6. The Savior had companions and followers, or his religion would have perished with him. Did these companions originate these fabulous stories? This is incredible, for they were better informed. Did they, then, leave no authentic account of their Master, either in writing or by tradition, so that all Christendom received as true the accounts given by persons entirely unauthorized?

7. It would have been the interest of the enemies of Jesus, no less than of his friends, to detect the error or the fraud that substituted a mythical and miraculous life of him for the truth. They are, however, not merely silent with regard to any error or fraud of the kind, but by explaining his miracles as wrought by magic, they imply an admission of the authenticity of the books that record them.

8. The Gentile Christians had received their faith from some early followers of Jesus. Would they have afterwards accepted as true an account of their Master's life made up not from actual facts, but from Jewish fancies?

9. The Christian religion, whether divinely revealed or not, is a sublime and beautiful whole, the representation of a perfect character, and an incomparable system of morals. Was this system, which has been the admiration of the world for ages, formed by chance — a mere farrago of idle rumors?

10. In his "Life of Jesus for the German People," published in 1864, Dr. Strauss has modified his mythical theory to a considerable extent, in conformity with the views of the "Tübingen School," Dr. F. C. Baur, and others. He now regards the Gospels as having been composed later than he at first admitted; that of Matthew the earliest, Luke before A. D. 135, Mark afterwards, and John about A. D. 150, thus leaving a longer time for the production of mythical stories. He also admits, to some extent, conscious fiction on the part of the writers, at least of the author of the fourth Gospel. At the same time he recognizes, more fully than before, something distinct in the person and teaching of Jesus. He regards him as a most pure and holy being,

combining the best influences of all the world's previous culture, and excited to noble self-devotion by those passages in the prophets that speak of a suffering Messiah.

Upon these modifications of his system, and upon the views of the remarkable school on which they are founded, it is not necessary, in this brief volume, to say more than has already been observed. (See p. 68.) The genuineness and authenticity of the Gospels being proved, we have all that is needed. The change of opinion in Dr. Strauss prepares us for further changes; and we trust that he or his successors may, ere long, be led to acknowledge in Jesus, not only the providential, but the divinely commissioned Leader of mankind.

The argument against the mythical theory is thus expressed in the same discourse, from which an extract has already been given (see p. 25) :—

"The legendary and the mythical history of Greece and Rome cannot be traced up, in written form, to within five hundred years of the time to which the events are ascribed. But here is the history of our Lord, which, if mythical, is the most wonderful of all myths, distinctly traced to four writers, who were living at the time, and who wrote and published their tales during the lifetime of many eye-witnesses of Jesus's ministry — a history perfectly self-consistent in its details, filled with miracle, and crowning them all with the miracle of a character claiming to be exalted in a degree hitherto unconceived; claiming to be the Son of God; claiming to be the future Judge of the world; the Lord, not only of life and death, but of the living and the dead; the arbiter of our eternal destiny; and this claim supported by a character so spotless that it has commanded the adoring veneration of all men from that day to this. And will any man attempt to persuade me that this wonderful, this unapproachable majesty and beauty, this self-consistent portrait of the Son of God, living and teaching and dying, in Galilee and Judea, was the creation of rumor, and popular fancy, and religious aspiration, created and made a living reality to thousands of believers, during the short space of thirty years intervening between the crucifixion of Jesus and the publication of his biographies? I should regard the attempt as almost an insult to my understanding. As reasonably might one attempt to persuade me that the strength of will and inflexibility of purpose ascribed to the old hero who occupied the executive chair of our nation thirty years ago was the pure creation of fancy during my own lifetime."

THE OLD TESTAMENT.

SECTION 26. GENERAL VIEW.

THE New Testament is the foundation of the faith of Christians. The Old Testament is of value to us as containing the records of God's dealings with man, in a revelation preliminary to that by Jesus Christ. It is sustained by the testimony of the New, and yields it support in turn.

It is sustained by the testimony of the New, because, —

1. Our Savior and his apostles frequently quote or refer to the Old Testament as of divine authority. (See Matt. xxii. 43 ; xxvi. 24 ; Luke xviii. 31 ; John v. 39.)

2. The position which Jesus claimed, as the Christ, or the Messiah, was that predicted by the Old Testament prophets.

The Old Testament sustains the New, —

1. By direct prophecies, which received their accomplishment in Christ.

2. By the proofs which the Old exhibits of divine origin and authority for the religion it makes known, joined to the indications it gives of being imperfect and temporary, and therefore preparatory to a more permanent system.

The Old Testament presents a system of faith and morals not unworthy of a divine origin.

1. Its first principle is the Unity of God ; and this is asserted in marked contrast to the idolatry which

prevailed throughout the world, and especially in Egypt, the country from which the Israelites came forth. (Gen. i.; Deut. vi. 4; 1 Chron. xvi. 26.)

2. In equally strong contrast with Egyptian superstition, which worshipped its divinities under bestial forms, it forbade the use of any visible representation of the Deity. (Ex. xx. 4.)

3. The very name which it gave to the Supreme, Jehovah, signifies "He is," or "the Self-existent." (See Ex. iii. 15, in the original, where the divine name is evidently the verb of existence in the third person, as in verse 14 it is in the first person.)

4. The invisible and spiritual nature of God, and his superiority to human wants or changes, are strongly set forth in such passages as Deut. iv. 12–26; Ps. l. 8–13; Isaiah i. 10–17; Mal. iii. 6.

5. The moral attributes of God — his justice, mercy, and beneficence — are declared in numerous passages, such as Ex. xxxiv. 6, 7; Ps. ciii. His power and wisdom in creating, and his providence in sustaining the universe, are constantly acknowledged. (See Gen. i.; Ps. civ.)

6. The laws given to the Israelites are of consummate wisdom. The Ten Commandments, especially, form a most comprehensive code, which still, after the lapse of thousands of years, and the increased light given by Christianity, retains the admiration and reverence of mankind. (Ex. xx.; Deut. v. 6–21.)

7. The laws relating to the treatment by the people of their poorer brethren were most wise and humane. (See Deut. xxiv. 6–22.) And although benevolence towards foreigners was not so strongly inculcated, — the

law of universal brotherhood being the especial glory of the Christian revelation, — yet in some passages the Old Testament makes a near approach to it. (Ex. xxii. 21; xxiii. 9.)

8. Even those defective institutions which, in that early stage of human progress, it was thought best not to prohibit entirely, were placed under restraints which greatly diminished their evils, and prepared the way for their entire removal. Thus it was with divorce (Deut. xxiv. 1–4; Mark x. 4, 5), with private revenge (Num. xxxv. 9–34), and with slavery. (Ex. xxi. 1–6, 16, 20, 26, 27.)

9. In contrast to the surrounding idolatry, the worship of the Hebrews was not marked either with cruelty or impurity; and their religion was free from the superstitions connected with charms, incantations, omens, and astrology.

10. The Old Testament is replete with passages of unrivalled sublimity and beauty, especially when it dwells upon the majesty of God, and the wisdom manifested in his works. (Ps. xxiii., xxix., civ.; Job xxviii., xxxix.; Is. ii. 10–22; xl. 21–31; Jer. iv. 23–26.)

Section 27. Difficulties of the Old Testament.

Much has been said and written with regard to the obscurities and difficulties of the Old Testament. On this subject we offer these remarks: —

1. Obscurities and difficulties are to be expected in ancient documents, from the great difference in thought and manner of expression between far distant periods of human development.

2. It was customary with ancient writers to relate occurrences in a dramatic manner, giving not merely the result of a conversation, but imagining the very words that might have been used. (See the remarks on the language of Herodotus, in Macaulay's Essay on History.) This peculiarity of ancient writing will explain many passages in the Old Testament, in which the Almighty is represented as speaking, and especially as conversing with human beings. (Gen. i. 3; ii. 16; Ex. xxxii. 7–14.)

3. In many of the narratives of the Old Testament, the account rests, not on the authority of the sacred historian, but on that of some earlier writer, or of tradition. Thus the occurrences recorded in Genesis could not be related by Moses from personal knowledge; and he, if he was the historian, is therefore not accountable for anything more than a faithful use of the materials he possessed. The account in Joshua x. 12–14 is there spoken of as derived from the Book of Jasher, which was apparently a collection of poems. (Compare 2 Sam. i. 18.)

4. If errors in astronomy, geology, or any other branch of science are discovered, it is to be remembered that the object of a revelation was not to teach men those sciences, but their own relation to their Creator.

5. If we find much to condemn in the conduct of persons who are yet mentioned with approval in the Old Testament, we must remember that they may have been approved for one quality, though in other respects very deficient. Thus David is spoken of, in 1 Sam. xiii. 14, as a "man after God's own heart" in the one respect of faithfulness to the divine commands in the administration of public affairs.

6. In judging such characters, we have also to bear in mind the lower standard of morals in their age, and the temptations to which they were peculiarly exposed. Thus, to recur to the instance just spoken of, David is to be judged, not by the modern and Christian standard, but as compared with men of his time, and subject, like him, to the temptations arising from the possession of despotic power.

7. If the sentiment of the historian himself appear incorrect, we must remember that good, and even inspired men, who lived before the time of Christ, had not that full view of duty which he afterwards communicated. (Matt. xi. 11.) To suppose that the most gifted of the prophets anticipated all that Christ had to teach would be to make Christ's teaching superfluous.

8. Even if doubt were cast upon some of the Old Testament books, as regards their genuineness or authenticity, such doubt would not seriously affect the claims of the Jewish religion to divine authority, and still less those of Christianity. The great facts would still remain of the Israelites' rescue from Egyptian bondage, and of their maintaining for centuries the worship of the One True God, in a world elsewhere filled with idolatry.

9. The free investigations of recent critics, while, as has been seen, they do not destroy the evidence on which the Jewish religion rests, sometimes incidentally remove objections against it. (See Colenso, "The Pentateuch and Book of Joshua," Part I. section 172.)

10. There appears in some writers a disposition to represent the Jewish religion as on a level with the heathenism of surrounding nations. Thus the impression is

given that the Jews regarded Jehovah as the God of their own nation, not the God of all mankind, in contradiction to the account in Gen. i., which represents him as the Creator of all, and numerous other passages. (See Deut. xxxii. 8; 2 Kings xix. 17–19; Ps. xcvi. 5; Isa. lxvi. 18–21.) In the same spirit, the attempt has been made, from Gen. xxii., to prove that the religion of the Hebrews sanctioned human sacrifices. As the sacrifice was in that case forbidden, the inference should be precisely the opposite.

We conclude this section with the following tribute to the excellence of the Hebrew system, by an eminent writer, who did not acknowledge its divine authority: "This must be confessed, that under the guidance of divine Providence, the great and beautiful doctrine of one God seems very early embraced by the great Jewish lawgiver, incorporated into his national legislation, defended with rigorous enactions, and slowly communicated to the world. At our day it is difficult to understand the service rendered to the human race by the mighty soul of Moses, and that a thousand years before Anaxagoras. His name is ploughed into the history of the world. His influence can never die. It must have been a vast soul, endowed with moral and religious genius to a degree extraordinary among men, which at that early age could attempt to found a state on the doctrine and worship of one God." (Parker's Discourse of Religion, p. 59.)

SECTION 28. EVIDENCE FOR THE OLD TESTAMENT.

The books of the Old Testament are sustained, in regard to their genuineness and authenticity, by internal and external evidence, as are those of the New Testament.

I. The external evidence is, —

1. The testimony of the Jewish nation, by which these books have been for ages acknowledged and valued, as containing the ancient records of their race, and the history of divine communications made to them.

They have, in fact, been regarded with a veneration, and preserved with a care, which may appear excessive and superstitious; great attention being paid to the slightest minutiæ of spelling and punctuation, the transcribers not venturing even to correct obvious errors in these respects, as they supposed that every variation was intended to indicate some mystery.

2. The Christian Scriptures, even if considered merely as works dating from the early ages of Christianity, prove, by numerous references and quotations, the existence of the Old Testament at that time, and substantially in the same form as at present.

3. Josephus, a Jewish commander and writer, who was taken prisoner by the Romans about A. D. 68, and afterwards received into favor by them, gives a history of his nation, and other writings, which are founded on the Old Testament, and constantly corroborate its accounts.

4. Similar testimony is given, though to a less extent, by Philo, a learned Jew of Alexandria, about the time of our Savior.

5. The Apocryphal books, written mostly by Alexandrian Jews, shortly before the Christian era, testify, by frequent references and constant implication, to the existence of the Old Testament writings, and their reception as of the highest authority among the nation.

6. The Samaritans, a race closely allied to the Jews, and still existing, though in very scanty numbers, confirm the Old Testament accounts by their traditions; and particularly by their possessing copies of the Pentateuch, or first five books of the Bible, in Hebrew, but written in peculiar characters, different from the common Hebrew letters, and supposed by some to be more ancient. The testimony of the Samaritans is the more valuable, as the jealousy which existed for centuries between them and the Jews would have rendered it impossible for any document of recent origin to be imposed upon them by their neighbors and rivals.

7. Various testimonies from heathen writers, and from ancient inscriptions, confirm statements of the Old Testament with regard to historical events. This description of evidence has been well exhibited in Rawlinson's "Bampton Lectures" (London, 1859), from which the following statements are selected: —

"Hecatæus of Abdera, Manetho, Lysimachus of Alexandria, Eupolemus, Tacitus, Juvenal, Longinus, ascribe to Moses the institution of that code of laws by which the Jews were distinguished from other nations; and the majority distinctly note that he committed his laws to writing." Of these, the first two were contemporary with Alexander the Great, in the fourth century before Christ. Longinus does not mention Moses by name, but as "the legislator of the Jews," quoting Gen. i. 3

as an instance of sublimity. (Rawlinson, pp. 43, 329–331.)

In the Bhagavat, an ancient Hindoo poem, the Lord of the universe speaks thus to Satiavrata: "In seven days from the present time, O thou tamer of enemies, the three worlds will be plunged in an ocean of death; but in the midst of the destroying waves, a large vessel, sent by me for thy use, shall stand before thee. Then shalt thou take all medicinal herbs, all the variety of seeds, and accompanied by seven saints, encircled by pairs of all brute animals, thou shalt enter the spacious ark, and continue in it, secure from the flood, on one immense ocean without light, except the radiance of thy holy companions." (p. 344.)

A similar account is given by Berosus, the Chaldean historian, of Xisuthrus, in which the incident of the sending forth of birds is related, as in Gen. viii. (p. 63.)

Manetho, the Egyptian historian, and Berosus, the Chaldean, present records of the ancient dynasties that were said to have governed their respective countries; and while they ascend to an antiquity far beyond that recorded in the Bible, this relates alone to a period of fabulous gods and heroes. When they reach the time of legitimate history, their dates correspond nearly with those of the Hebrew Scriptures. (pp. 57–60.)

Three ancient authors, Moses of Chorene, Procopius, and Suidas, relate that there existed in their times, at Tingis, or Tangiers, in Africa, an ancient inscription, to the effect that the inhabitants were descendants of those fugitives who were driven from the land of Canaan by Joshua, the son of Nun, the plunderer. (pp. 91, 92.)

Nicolaus of Damascus, the friend of Augustus Cæsar,

gives, from the records of his native city, an account of the war of the ancient king, Hadad, with David, king of Judea, confirming the account in 2 Sam. viii. 5, 6. (p. 95.)

In 1 Kings xvi. 31, we are told that Ahab "took to wife Jezebel, the daughter of Ethbaal, king of the Zidonians." In the Tyrian history of Menander we are told that Eithobalus, priest of Ashteroth, became king of Tyre by murdering his predecessor, at a time which exactly agrees with this statement. We are also told that, during the reign of this prince, a remarkable drought occurred in Phœnicia, which continued for a year. (See 1 Kings xvii. 1; xviii. 1–5; Rawlinson, p. 127.) The priestly office held by Eithobalus, and the crime by which he gained his power, coincide with the blending of idolatrous fanaticism and bloody ambition in his daughter Jezebel and his granddaughter Athaliah. (1 Kings xviii. 4; xxi. 5–15; 2 Kings viii. 18, 26; xi. 1, 18.)

The scriptural accounts of Pharaoh Necho (2 Kings xxiii. 29–35; Jer. xlvi. 2), and Pharaoh Hophra (Jer. xliv. 30), are confirmed by Manetho and Herodotus. (pp. 148, 149.)

Events in sacred history are also confirmed in a very interesting manner by the recently deciphered inscriptions on the monuments of Egypt, and on those which have been discovered at Nineveh and other Assyrian cities.

The conquest of Rehoboam by Shishak, king of Egypt (1 Kings xiv. 25, 26), "is found to have been commemorated by Shishak on the outside of the great temple at Karnac; and here, in a long list of captured towns and districts, which Shishak boasts of having added to his dominions, occurs the 'Melchi Yudah,' or kingdom of Judah." (pp. 125, 126.)

"The separate existence of the two kingdoms of Israel and Judah is abundantly confirmed by the Assyrian inscriptions. Kings of each country occur in the accounts which the great Assyrian monarchs have left us of their conquests, the names being always capable of easy identification with those recorded in Scripture, and occurring in the chronological order which is there given." (p. 125.)

The reign of Ben-hadad at Damascus, his military power, and even the peculiar construction of his armies (1 Kings xx. 1, 25), are illustrated by Assyrian inscriptions. (pp. 130, 407.) On the same monument Hazael appears as successor to Ben-hadad; and Jehu is mentioned as king of Israel at the same date.

The intervention of Tiglath-Pileser in behalf of Ahaz against the united forces of Syria and Israel (2 Kings xvi. 7) is confirmed in the same manner. The erection by Ahaz of a Syrian, or rather Assyrian, altar at Jerusalem (verse 10), is explained by the inscriptions, from which it appears that it was customary to require subject nations thus to acknowledge the gods of the conquerors. (p. 136.)

The subjugation of Hezekiah by Sennacherib (2 Kings xviii. 13) is confirmed by a long inscription, agreeing with the scriptural account in every particular, except that it states the tribute in silver at a higher amount. That in gold is precisely the same — thirty talents. (p. 141.)

We are told, in 2 Chron. xxiii. 11, that the king of Assyria took Manasseh king of Judah captive, and carried him to Babylon. This statement appears strange, as Nineveh was the capital of Assyria, and we know Babylon in connection with a later empire. But the inscriptions show us that Esar-haddon, the monarch in question, and he only of all the Assyrian kings, built a palace at Babylon, and occasionally held his court there. Manasseh is mentioned among his subject princes. (p. 145.)

The king of Egypt, whose name is given as So in our translation, would, with different vowel-points, which are a comparatively modern addition, be recognized as Sevech. This monarch appears both in Manetho and in the Egyptian inscriptions, and his connection with Assyrian history is confirmed by the discovery of his seal at Koyunjik, in Assyria. (2 Kings xvii. 4. Rawlinson, p. 147.)

In Daniel v., Belshazzar is named as the last king of Babylon, and as having been slain when the city was taken by the Medes and Persians. This statement long appeared to be contrary to that of profane historians, who named Nabonadius as the last king, and declared that he was absent from Babylon at the time of its occupation by the enemy, and that he was afterwards taken prisoner, and treated with generosity. But in 1854 the discovery was made, from inscriptions at Mugheir, the ancient "Ur of the Chaldees," that Nabonadius had associated with him in the sovereignty a son whose name corresponds with the account in Daniel. (pp. 168–170.)

II. The Internal Evidence of the Old Testament is found in the agreement of the statements and references there with what is known from other sources of the history, geography, and antiquities of Palestine and neighboring countries; in coincidences between the books, especially where they are obviously undesigned; and in the general simple, truthful style of the narrative. For example, the history of the deliverance from Egypt, and of the wanderings in the wilderness, exhibits a perfect acquaintance on the part of the writer with the geography of the region where the scene is laid; so that the route of the Israelites may be readily traced by the traveller. The Red Sea, at the point where the Israelites are described to have crossed, is a narrow and shallow sound, where the concurrence of a strong wind and an ebb tide might facilitate such a passage.

Much of the history is given in two accounts, the books of Chronicles confirming the statements in those of Samuel and Kings.

There are numerous coincidences between the historical books and the prophecies and psalms. (Compare, for instance, Judges ix. 53 with 2 Sam. xi. 21; Josh. xviii. 1 with Jer. vii. 12; 2 Kings iii. 27 with Amos ii. 1.)

The argument from Institutions, as shown in a previous section (see p. 34), is applicable to the religion of the Old Testament, as well as to that of the New. The Passover, still observed among the Jews, bears witness to the deliverance from Egypt; and numerous other observances, whether now maintained or not, but well known to have been observed before the destruction of the temple, testify to the truth of those Scriptures which alone explain their origin. (See this argument further developed in Leslie's "Short Method with Deists.")

It is not necessary, however, in this brief summary, to dwell further on particulars of this nature. To Christians, the great evidence for the authority of the Old Testament is that derived from its connection with the New; and for questions of Old Testament criticism, regarding the authorship of books, or correctness of historical accounts, so far as they do not affect the acknowledgment of the Jewish law as of divine origin, Christianity is not responsible.

SECTION 29. OLD TESTAMENT PROPHECY.

An important branch of the Evidences of Christianity is derived from the fulfilment of prophecy. In considering this, we view first the Prophecies of the Old Testament fulfilled in the New.

Independently of especial predictions, the history of the Jews, with that of their thoughts and feelings, possesses a prophetical character.

Other nations have fixed their ideal of human existence in the past. The Greeks and Romans held that there had been a golden age, when mankind were pure and happy. The Hebrews shared this view only in reference to the primitive happiness and innocence of the Garden of Eden. When that brief period was at an end their imagination turned towards the future.

All through the Jewish history there appears an anticipation of a glorious Ruler, to be sent by Heaven, and of a happy and virtuous state. This anticipation not only appears in occasional passages, but it became interwoven with the thoughts of the people; so that about the time of the Christian era, the expectation of such a ruler was general, not only in Judea, but in the surrounding nations. This we have on the authority of the Jewish historian Josephus, and of the Romans Suetonius and Tacitus. (See Josephus, Bell. Jud. vi. 5, § 4; Suetonius, Vita Vespasiani, § 4; Tacitus, Hist., § 13.

This expectation was so strongly fixed in the mind of

the Jewish race, that it remained after their rejection of the claims of Jesus, has survived the disappointments, wanderings, and sufferings of eighteen hundred years, and is still cherished by their descendants to this day.

While they looked forward to this personage, whom they called the Messiah, as a conquering king, they also anticipated that he would restore the national purity of worship.

At the same time, they found passages in their prophetical books inconsistent with the idea of his uninterrupted success — passages intimating a ministry of suffering. Hence some of their writers assert that there will be two Messiahs; one the son of David, a royal conqueror; the other the son of Ephraim, a suffering reformer. (See Strauss's Life of Jesus, Part III., ch. i. § 112.)

Such are the indications of the Old Testament, according to the interpretation put upon it by the race who received it as divinely communicated.

At the age of the world when the expectation of a Messiah was most active in the minds of men, a person appeared whose character and history corresponded to this expectation. He is represented to have been a descendant of David. Although not literally a king, he called the community he established a kingdom; and the term was justified by the greatness of the power his teachings exercised. Although not literally a conqueror, his cause has triumphed over the opposition of monarchs and of nations, and now exerts its control over the civilized world.

The predictions of a suffering Messiah have been fulfilled more literally, for Jesus endured poverty, reproach, abandonment, and betrayal, and finally laid down his life in the cause of his religion.

If it be objected that the character in which Jesus appeared was not that of a triumphant king in which he was foretold, and that on this account he was rejected by his own nation, who were best qualified to judge of his claims, we reply, —

1. That it is essential to the character of prophecy that it should not indicate its accomplishment with perfect clearness. If it did, the fulfilment would appear to have been brought about by studied effort.

2. The reasons of the rejection of Jesus by his countrymen are apparent. The nation was eager for deliverance from the Roman yoke, and looked for the Messiah to lead them to this object. They rejected, therefore, the claims of a peaceful, spiritual Messiah. Joined to their disappointment on this account was the opposition of the ruling classes to all attempts at reform — an opposition greatly embittered by Jesus' bold denunciation of their prevalent vices.

3. While the Jews were thus prejudiced by their national feelings against the claims of Jesus, they had an answer to the evidence of miracles which would not be sanctioned by the philosophy of our day. It does not appear, either from the New Testament or from the Jewish or heathen writers, that they ever denied the reality of the miracles; but they asserted that these were wrought by the power of evil spirits. (See Matt. xii. 24; Luke xi. 15; John viii. 48.)

4. The chief reason, named above, for which the Jews rejected the claims of Jesus, is to us a strong proof in favor of those claims. He fulfilled the prophecies in a

higher sense than the prophets themselves probably were able to grasp. His nation, in the worldliness of their views, were disappointed in him; but we, at this distance of time, can perceive their error. The station which the Savior has held, for ages after ages, as spiritual king of numerous nations, and as the guide of mankind in the path of virtue, — to say nothing of any supremacy he may exercise hereafter in the future life, — is far higher than the glory of a conquering king of Palestine. This thought, of the superiority of his spiritual dominion to a kingdom like that of David, he suggested in the form of a question, but found no response. (Matt. xxii. 45.)

5. Yet it is scarce conceivable that a Jew, in that age of formal observances and low morality, should (except by divine revelation) have entertained the idea of fulfilling the prophecies in this higher sense; that he should have believed the predictions, and that he was the person to whom they pointed, yet should have refused to tread the path of military adventure, which all around expected him to tread, incurring thus the danger of a shameful death; and that by this strange path he should actually have succeeded in his bold aspirations.

6. It may be further remarked, that the idea being imparted to the prophets, by revelation, of a leader and reformer, divinely sent and consecrated, they would of necessity imagine him to occupy the station which would seem most dignified and most favorable for his task — the station of king and conqueror.

7. We are taught, by indications in the prophets themselves, that predictions are sometimes conditional, and that their fulfilment may be prevented by the

unworthiness of those to whom a promise is made; or by their repentance, if the prophecy be a threat. (See Jer. xviii. 7–10; Jonah iii. 10; iv. 11.) We can conceive that if the Jews had accepted Jesus as the Messiah, the prophecies respecting him might have been fulfilled in their lower sense as well as in their higher. The gentle spirit of his religion might have prevented the rebellion which led to their national overthrow; the gospel might have spread with great rapidity; and Jesus, without directly interfering with established monarchies, might have ruled them all. Admitting that the divine promise was to be understood in a strictly literal sense, we see how it might have been fulfilled, had it not been forfeited by the national rejection of Jesus.

The above argument, from the Jews' expectation of the Messiah, and the fulfilment of it by Jesus, would have force, even if every prophecy now applied to him were proved to have had some other application. For the questions would still occur, How came the Jewish people to anticipate a Messiah? and How, without divine intervention, was this anticipation met by the coming of one who should save and rule not only Israel, but the human race? The expectation and its fulfilment fit into each other as parts of the same whole.

Section 30. The Jewish Revelation prophetic of the Christian.

Again, the Jewish revelation is a prophecy of the Christian.

The Jewish religion possesses, as we have seen (p. 91), strong claims to a divine origin. It teaches the unity and other attributes of God, which all the surrounding nations denied; it teaches a much purer morality than theirs; its documents, which have evidently come down from a very high antiquity, and its tradition, confirmed by that of the rival branch, the Samaritans, agree in testifying to ancient divine manifestations, revealing the truths it teaches. But the Jewish religion alone is incomplete, deficient. Many of its instructions are evidently intended for the tribes to whom it was originally given, not for all mankind. It prescribes a ritual service, to be performed in one place, to which the people were required to resort three times a year (Ex. xxiii. 17), and forbids altars to be erected for sacrifice elsewhere. These and other regulations are evidently national. In some laws, too, the object plainly was, to keep the people apart from other nations. Thus the complicated distinctions between clean and unclean meats, and other rules relating to ceremonial purity, rendered it difficult for Jews to live on terms of familiar intercourse with foreigners. (Lev. xi.) By such laws commerce was discouraged, while agriculture was cherished by regulations for the tenure of land, which it was made impossible for any family permanently to alienate. (Lev. xxv. 10, 23–34.)

Even if it were admitted that many or most of these rules were of more recent date than has generally been assigned to them, we have reason to suppose that their spirit was in accordance with the known customs and tendency of the nation. So too if it were admitted that the books ascribed to Moses were of later origin than his time, the general substance of the account they give must still be in accordance with national traditions. No man could impose upon a people an entirely false account of their own origin, and of the derivation and meaning of all their public observances, for the humblest citizen would be able to contradict him. (See p. 33.)

Three suppositions may be formed to account for the existence of the Jewish religion.

I. That it was the growth of human thought.

II. That it was revealed from above as a system complete and permanent.

III. That it was revealed from above as a system preparatory to a fuller revelation.

1. The first supposition implies the falsehood of all the historical and traditional accounts, so far as they involve anything of miracle. It implies, therefore, that those who taught this system were guilty of imposture on the largest scale. The peculiar purity and nobleness of the system render it difficult to believe this respecting its authors. As we look upon the whole world lying in the darkness of idolatry, and one only nation worshipping the living and true God, we naturally recognize this exception, not as the result of vile fraud and jugglery, but as designed by God to keep alive the remembrance of truth upon the earth.

2. The second supposition is inconsistent with what we have pointed out as the temporary and limited characteristics of the system. It was designed for a single nation; and, so far from encouraging them to become teachers of the truth to others, it kept them from intercourse with others by jealous restrictions. It taught the brotherhood of all Israelites, but said little of the brotherhood of mankind; and this though it held within itself, in its account of the common origin of man, the

germ of a more comprehensive liberality. So, though it taught the Unity of God, it announced him as especially the God of Abraham and his descendants.

3. These limitations of the system show its preparatory character. It was from above, but was not the last nor the best gift of Heaven. Its character as a local religion showed that a universal one was yet to come; its character as a ceremonial system betokened the future approach of one which should be spiritual.

And Christianity fulfils this promise of its predecessor. It does no dishonor to the Jewish system; accepts it as divine, so far as it goes; but goes beyond it, and renders it complete. Without Christianity we could not account for God's giving a system so glorious, yet so imperfect, as Judaism. Without Judaism we could not account for the fact that God withheld from the world, for so many ages, the light of Christianity.

The period when that light was given, and the circumstances which accompanied it, indicate, by their appropriateness, the agency of divine wisdom. It was when the Jewish observances had lost much of their spiritual life, and become debased to formalism and bigotry, and when the heathen systems around had, to a great extent, lost their hold on the faith of the nations that yet outwardly maintained them. The tribes of the East had been brought together into one political family by the conquests of Alexander the Great, and those of the West by the conquests of the Romans; while the final ascendency of the latter had combined the whole in one great empire, throughout which two languages, — and those nearly related to each other, — the Greek and the Latin, were generally understood. The brilliant period of heathen philosophy was past, so that its rivalship to the new religion was little to be dreaded; and the long and bloody civil wars of the Roman empire had been closed by the triumph of Augustus. Then, too, the successive invaders of Palestine had carried thence multitudes of captive Jews, and had settled them in the principal cities of Asia Minor, Greece, and Italy; so that there was everywhere the material for forming the nucleus of a Christian church. Thus, by divine appointment, the conquests of ambitious men and the pride of philosophy were overruled for the extension of the great blessing that was about to be given to the world.

If it be objected that these favorable circumstances, instead of proving the care of Providence for the spread of the truth, should rather be regarded as sufficient to account for the spread of an imposture, the reply is easy. These same circumstances, of intellectual light and profound peace, while they would favor the diffusion of truth, would be unfavorable to that of falsehood, for they would render its detection easier. The existence of a Jewish community in every city not only gave the Christian teachers the means of obtaining their first hearing, but it gave their opponents also the means of answering them, so far as any answer could be given. Deceit prospers best in darkness, but the light was favorable to Christianity because it was the truth.

If it still be questioned why this blessing of a true religion was so long withheld from all the world except Palestine, we reply that both sacred and profane history afford indications of an earlier revelation than that given by Moses; and from this primitive communication was probably derived much of the spiritual knowledge which the heathens possessed. This knowledge became corrupted by polytheism, and afterwards weakened by scepticism; and then it was that the new and full revelation was bestowed.

SECTION 31. INDIVIDUAL PROPHECIES OF THE OLD TESTAMENT.

The prophetic passages of the Old Testament which are adduced in proof of its sacred claims are partly those which had their fulfilment before Christ, and partly those which received their accomplishment in him.

Of the former class we shall present some instances, in predictions of the desolation of cities and regions which were strong and prosperous at the time when these predictions were made. The fulfilment of these prophecies is evident to every one who travels in the East, or who reads the accounts presented by such travellers of the desolation of once populous countries, and the ruin of once proud capitals. Such predictions respecting Nineveh may be found in Nahum i. 9, Zeph. ii. 13, 15; respecting Moab, in Zeph. ii. 8, 9, Jer. xlviii. 42; respecting Philistia, in Zeph. ii. 4. The fate of Edom is foretold in Jer. xlix. 16–18; a prophecy the fulfilment of which was made evident only recently by the discovery of the ruins of Petra, the rock-built capital of Edom. Respecting Egypt, see Ezek. xxix. 15, xxx. 13; respecting Tyre, Ezek. xxvi. 4, 5; and with regard to Babylon, Is. xiii. 20, 21.

There are many passages in the Old Testament which have been understood as prophetic of the Savior. Indeed, some theologians have been fond of recognizing not only the language, but the characters, of the Jewish state, as prefiguring the events of the New Dispensation. Thus David, Solomon, and others have been represented as types of Christ.

We cannot wonder at this, when we examine such a portion of Scripture as the seventy-second psalm. This bears, as its title (of whatever authority the title may be), "For Solomon;" and to a great extent it seems applicable to him. But there are verses that cannot be applied to any temporal sovereign with propriety. (See verses 5, 7, 11, 17.) These, therefore, have been supposed to refer to the Messiah. The usual explanation has been, that Solomon was a type of Christ, and that some things were said of him in that character which were not true of him as an earthly prince.

Another view of the subject is the following: The prophetic insight into the future had, of course, its limits. The prophets knew that there was to be a glorious personage, whom they contemplated chiefly under the character of the Messiah, or Anointed, — that is, the King. They knew not, however, generally speaking, in what age he was to appear. Each of them, therefore, while foretelling the glories of some monarch's reign, and indulging the hope that he might be the Messiah, would be led to blend with the nearer prospect the vast but less definite perspective of the future age of glory. Thus traits which belong to the Messiah are blended in the second psalm with an inauguration ode; in the forty-fifth with a marriage hymn; in the psalm now before us with a song of congratulation; in Is. vii., xi., and other passages, with predictions of the times of Hezekiah; and perhaps in Daniel ix. with what related primarily to the age of the Maccabees.

It will not materially affect the value of prophetical evidence if we adopt a wider or a stricter theory of prophetical foreknowledge. Whether any particular writer was himself inspired to foretell future events, or whether he only gave utterance to the national anticipation, derived from divine communications in ages past, his declarations will alike remain proofs of the Messiahship of Jesus, convincing in proportion to the clearness with which the reality answered to the prediction.

We subjoin some of the most remarkable prophecies, which appear to have received their fulfilment in Jesus Christ.

Genesis xxii. 18. "In thy seed shall all the nations of the earth be blessed." The hopes of those rude ages were generally fixed on the conquest of other tribes, not on conferring blessings. The promise that looks to such a privilege betokens a wider foresight than that of an ancient chief. It is finding its fulfilment in the progress of Christianity, and could not possibly find it in any other.

Psalm xxii. In this psalm the following sentences are most observable. The first words, quoted by the Savior on the cross, "My God, my God, why hast thou forsaken me?" were probably not, as used by him, an exclamation of distrust, but an application of the psalm to himself. Verses 7, 8. "All they that see me laugh me to scorn; they shoot out the lip, they shake the head, saying, He trusted on the Lord that he would deliver him; let him deliver him, seeing he delighted in him." Verse 16. "The assembly of the wicked have enclosed me; they pierced my hands and my feet." Verse 18. "They part my garments among them, and cast lots upon my vesture." The coincidence of the sixteenth verse with the sufferings of Christ is the more remarkable as the punishment of crucifixion was unknown among the Jews of the age when the psalm was written.

Psalm cx. 4. "The Lord hath sworn, and will not repent, Thou art a priest forever after the order of Melchizedek," that is, a priest of an entirely different order from that of Aaron — a kingly priest, and one without predecessor or successor in his office, as the expression is explained in Heb. vii. This psalm is not the less a prophecy of the Messiah because it portrays him according to Jewish ideas as a conquering monarch. If the prophets had understood and declared the full spiritual glory of the revelation that was to come, there would have been nothing left for that revelation to communicate.

Isaiah ix. 6. "For unto us a child is born, unto us a son is given: and the government shall be upon his shoulder; and his name shall be called Wonderful, Counsellor, the mighty God, the everlasting Father, the Prince of Peace. Of the increase of his government and peace there shall be no end, upon the throne of David, and upon his kingdom, to order it, and to establish it with judgment and with justice from henceforth even forever. The zeal of the Lord of hosts will perform this." Some of the epithets admit of a different translation; but the passage still points to a greater monarch than any mere Jewish prince.

Isaiah xlix. 5, 6. "Though Israel be not gathered, yet shall I be glorious in the eyes of the Lord, and my God shall be my strength. And he said, It is a light thing that thou shouldest be my servant to raise up the tribes of Jacob, and to restore the preserved of Israel: I will also give thee for a light to the Gentiles, that thou mayest be my salvation unto the ends of the earth." In this passage the prophet penetrates farther into the future than at other times, and recognizes the Messiah rejected by the Jews, but invested with higher glory as the Redeemer of mankind. (See also chapter lx.)

Isaiah lii. 13, to liii. 12. This remarkable passage is referred to, as prophetic of the Savior, in Acts viii. 32. The appropriateness of this application is evident in the common version, particularly in the 5th, 6th, and 7th verses. "He was wounded for our transgressions, he was bruised for our iniquities; the chastisement of our peace was upon him, and with his stripes we are healed. All we, like sheep, have gone astray; we have turned every one to his own way; and the Lord hath laid on him the iniquity of us all. He was oppressed, and he was afflicted, yet he opened not his mouth: he is brought as a lamb to the slaughter, and as a sheep before her shearers is dumb, so he openeth not his mouth." Some verses, however, acquire a clearer application in the translation of Dr. Noyes, as verses 8–10: —

"By oppression and punishment he was taken away;
And who of that generation would consider,
That he was cut off from the land of the living,
That for the transgression of my people he was smitten?
His grave was appointed with the wicked,
And with the rich man was his sepulchre,
Although he had done no injustice,
And there was no deceit in his mouth.
It pleased Jehovah severely to bruise him;
But since he gave himself a sacrifice for sin,
He shall see posterity; he shall prolong his days,
And the pleasure of Jehovah shall prosper in his hand."

In this passage we have the ideas of suffering patiently endured for the sake of others; of condemnation, execution, and burial; and, notwithstanding all these, of life continued, usefulness, and glory.

Micah v. 2. "But thou, Beth-lehem Ephratah, though thou be little among the thousands of Judah, yet out of thee shall he come forth unto me that is to be ruler in Israel; whose goings forth have been from of old, from everlasting." (See Matt. ii. 5, 6.)

Haggai ii. 7, 9. "I will shake all nations, and the desire of all nations shall come: and I will fill this house with glory, saith the Lord of hosts." "The glory of this latter house shall be greater than of the former, saith the Lord of hosts: and in this place will I give peace, saith the Lord of hosts."

Malachi iii. i. "Behold, I will send my messenger, and he shall prepare the way before me; and the Lord, whom ye seek, shall suddenly come to his temple, even the messenger of the covenant, whom ye delight in; behold, he shall come, saith the Lord of hosts." (See Matt. xi. 10.)

Malachi iv. 5, 6. "Behold, I will send you Elijah the prophet before the coming of the great and dreadful day of the Lord; and he shall turn the heart of the fathers to the children, and the heart of the children to their fathers, lest I come and smite the earth with a curse." (See Matt. xi. 14.) The last words of the Old dispensation are thus connected with the coming of that prophet who was the herald of the New.

Section 32. New Testament Prophecy, and subsequent History of the Jews.

I. Besides the proof of Christianity from prophecies in the Old Testament, which received their fulfilment in Christ, there is another, from predictions either by Jesus himself or his apostles, which have been fulfilled in subsequent events.

The most remarkable class of these is that of the predictions concerning the destruction of Jerusalem and the overthrow of the Jewish state. These are found at most length in Matt. xxiv., Mark xiii., Luke xvii. 20–37, xxi. Perhaps, however, they may appear in a still more striking form in some passages where they occur incidentally, and which bear so evidently the marks of the Savior's peculiar style, or of strong emotion, that we can hardly imagine them to be from any other source than his own lips. (See Matt. xxiii. 37–39; Luke xix. 41–44; xxiii. 28–31.)

The fulfilment of these prophecies is a matter of unquestionable notoriety. About thirty years after the crucifixion, the Jews rebelled against the Roman power. After a war waged with great ferocity on both sides, their capital was besieged, and suffered every extremity of distress from famine and from internal discord, as well as from the arms of the enemy. It was at length taken by assault, utterly destroyed, and the remnant of the people carried into captivity.

If it be objected that in some of the passages referred to indications are given of events which have not taken place, as of the visible return of Jesus to judgment, and of the end of the world, it is sufficient to answer, —

1. That many of the expressions are evidently highly figurative, and that the figures employed may allowably be supposed to mean nothing more than the rapid extension of the Christian religion, after the Jewish power, which oppressed it, had been broken down.

2. That, as the ancient prophets, in their visions, often blended the distant with the near, we need not be surprised to find that even our Savior did not distinctly mark the boundaries of time between the events of the approaching age and the final consummation.

II. As the Old Testament, in its general bearing, has been shown to be prophetic of the New, by its combined excellences and deficiencies, necessitating the coming of the system that was to perfect it, and thus proving its truth, so, apart from any direct prediction of our Savior, the events of his life and death necessitated the overthrow of the Jewish state, and his claims are confirmed by that catastrophe which fulfilled this implied prediction.

The Israelitish state had stood for fifteen hundred years. It had survived repeated conquest and captivity, and seemed as likely to endure, in its humble condition, as any other portion of the immense dominions of Rome. The conquerors were tolerant to national peculiarities of belief, and their power was so extensive that rebellion seemed madness. At this time Jesus appeared. He claimed to be the promised Messiah; but his claim was rejected, and himself cruelly put to death by the nation he addressed. If he was what he claimed to be, this rejection of him required the rejection of the nation in its turn, its loss of whatever peculiar privileges it had enjoyed before. This was due, both to retributive justice, and to the vindication of the Messiah's claims. If the Jewish state had stood uninjured for even a hundred years after the crucifixion of Jesus, the fact would have afforded a strong argument against his claim to a divine commission.

But the fact was otherwise. The great transgression received its punishment in the signal overthrow of the nation by whom it had been committed. The solemn ritual they boasted to have observed, with few intervals, since the days of Moses, was abolished, and has not, for near eighteen hundred years, been ever restored. In this event a strong providential confirmation was given to the authority of Jesus. We have reason to believe that it was so regarded in the age when it took place, and that no event contributed more to strengthen the faith of Christians, and to commend it to the reception of others, than this public vindication of the Redeemer's cause by that divine Providence that rules the affairs of nations.

It may be further observed, that the overthrow of the Jewish nation was in exact accordance with the threatenings, by their own prophets, of calamities that should come upon them if they neglected the law of God. (See Deut. xxviii.) But they had been extremely tenacious of that law, especially during the period preceding their final overthrow. They had not, therefore, committed the offence against which the penalty was denounced, unless it was in rejecting the claims of Jesus; and the fate that came upon them is unaccountable, except on that supposition. But if Jesus was such a prophet as was foretold in Deut. xviii. 15, then in rejecting him they transgressed the command, and incurred thereby their own rejection. (See verse 19. Acts iii. 22, 23.)

The history of the Jewish race, so remarkable in its previous stages, is not less so since that awful event which appeared to be its ruin. The very fact that it is yet existing seems a miracle; it is indeed a *moral miracle*, such as we have already pointed out in the existence and power of Christianity in the world. (See p. 25.) Other nations of that early period have passed away. The Romans, formerly so powerful, exist no longer; the tribes which once inhabited France, Spain, and Northern Africa, have left scarce a trace of their languages or their institutions. The Greeks, indeed, who, though subjected, were never actually driven from their soil, nor incorporated with its conquerors, still exist, and speak their ancient language in an altered form; but they profess a different religion from that of their ancestors. But the Jews, though their state was utterly overthrown, — though their race, driven from Palestine, was the object of cruel oppression, by Turk and Christian, in the various lands through which they were scattered, — yet exist, cherishing their ancient and peculiar language, and holding in reverence their venerable law. This fact, wonderful in itself, possesses the greater claim on our regard, as connected with predictions, both in the Old and New Testaments, whose fulfilment, in some manner unknown to us, may still, with reverence, be anticipated. The Jewish race is apparently preserved for some high purpose; perhaps that its final conversion to Christianity may establish, in clearer light than ever before, the divine authority of the gospel. (See Ezek. xxxvi. 25–38; Hosea iii. 5; Rom. xi. 25, 26.)

SECTION 33. MARTYRDOMS.

The evidence afforded, by the patient sufferings of the early Christians, to the truth of their religion, may be regarded in two aspects.

1. As furnishing proof of the sincerity of its early teachers, and thus of the truth of the accounts they gave.

2. As showing the excellence of the religion, and its divine authority, by the power it exhibited of sustaining its martyrs, and by the qualities of patience, submission, forgiveness to enemies, and hope of heaven, which it communicated to them.

I. In both these respects the sufferings of Jesus himself are first to be considered.

That these sufferings were endured by him in the manner recorded in the Gospels is confirmed to us by the absence of all evidence to the contrary. If the enemies of Jesus could with truth have asserted that he begged for his life, retracted his claims, or exhibited anything unworthy in language or in conduct, they would have eagerly proclaimed it; and we should at least find traces in the Gospels or Epistles of some controversy on the subject.

We have, then, the facts that the Founder of our religion endured a painful and shameful death, in consequence of his claims, and that he bore it with the most heroic fortitude, the meekest resignation, and the most touching exhibition of a forgiving spirit towards those by whose agency he suffered.

These facts show the sincerity of the sufferer. If he

had made claims which he knew to be false, he would have endeavored to escape by retracting them; or, if his own pride or the rage of his enemies had prevented this, the consciousness of guilt would have impaired his courage and composure. His prayer for the forgiveness of his enemies, and his words to the penitent thief (Luke xxiii. 43), would, then, have been the most blasphemons hypocrisy, counterfeiting to perfection the language of heavenly mercy and divine authority; and his last utterance, at the very point of death, "Father, into thy hands I commend my spirit," would have been bold mockery of the God before whom he was to appear. This, when taken in connection with all we know of his character and teachings, is utterly incredible.

II. The Christian religion derives a confirmation of its truth from the sufferings endured by its early preachers; for those preachers must have known the truth or falsehood of what they proclaimed. For instance, they universally declared that Jesus had risen from the dead, and many of them professed to have seen him after his resurrection. If this was not true, they were gross deceivers. Now, if they persevered in the account they gave, notwithstanding that it brought upon them obloquy, danger, and death, their constancy furnishes strong proof that they were true witnesses.

Of the fact of their sufferings we have, in the first place, a strong presumption from the nature of the case. They braved the hostility alike of Jews and Gentiles; of the Jews, by maintaining that the Teacher whom they had caused to be crucified was the Messiah, thus accusing the authorities of the nation of a sacrilegious murder; and of the Gentiles, by undertaking, in the name of this new Teacher, to subvert the established system of heathenism. If they were not persecuted under these circumstances, human nature must have been different in that age from what it has been at any period before or since.

We have, next, proof from Scripture history. That tells us that some of these early Christian teachers endured exile (Acts viii. 1), scourging (Acts v. 40; xvi. 23), imprisonment (Acts xii. 4; xxiv. 27), stoning (Acts xiv. 19), and distinctly records the violent death of two of their number (Acts vii. 59, 60; xii. 2), within twelve years from that of their Master.

We have next the testimony of Jewish and heathen writers. Josephus tells us of the martyrdom of the apostle James the Less. He says that in the interval between the death of the procurator Festus and the arrival of his successor, the High Priest Ananus caused James, "the brother of Jesus, who was called Christ," to be put to death by stoning. It is thought by some that the words we have particularly quoted were added in explanation by some transcriber; but there appears to be no reason to doubt the identity of the victim, as the account given by Eusebius, from Christian tradition, is nearly the same. (See Josephus, Antiq. xx. 9, § 1.)

Tacitus, who was born in the reign of Nero, about the middle of the first century, tells us that that Emperor, in order to turn from himself the suspicion of having set fire to the city of Rome, "laid the guilt, and inflicted the most cruel punishments, upon a set of people who were held in abhorrence for their crimes, and called, by the vulgar, Christians. Great numbers of these were put to death, with various torture, — some being disguised in the skins of beasts and worried to death by dogs, and others wrapped in pitched shirts, and set on fire at evening, that they might serve as torches to illuminate the night." (Annal. xv. 44.)

Suetonius, another writer of the same age, speaks of the persecution more briefly, and with equal ignorance of the character of those whom it affected. He says, only, " The Christians were punished — a set of men of a new and mischievous superstition." (Vita Neronis, § 16.)

The account of Tacitus is confirmed by Juvenal, a contemporaneous poet, and by Martial, who wrote somewhat later, both of whom refer to the horrible punishment of the pitched garment.

About seventy years after the resurrection, the younger Pliny (Caius Plinius Secundus), Governor of Bithynia and Pontus, wrote to the Emperor Trajan an account of the prevalence of Christianity in the provinces under his care, and of the measures taken for its suppression. The "superstition," according to him, had seized many of either sex and of every age; not in the cities only, but through the country, so that the temples of the gods were comparatively deserted. The profession of Christianity was a capital crime, and Pliny, though humanely disposed, had put to death many on account of it; but accusations continued to come in, many from anonymous sources; and the magistrate could not discover that the persons accused had been guilty of any criminal practices, except attendance on the rites of their faith. From the best that he could learn, too, these consisted only of prayer and singing, a simple banquet, and an exhortation to each other to avoid bad conduct. He writes, there-

fore, to the emperor, for further orders. The reply of Trajan approves his course, and directs him not to encourage informations, but to punish those who should be convicted and should refuse to retract. (Plin. Epist. x. 97.)

To turn from the evidence of their enemies to that of the Christians themselves, we have the following from Clement of Rome, one of the apostolical fathers: "Let us take the examples of our own age. Through zeal and envy, the most faithful and righteous pillars of the church have been persecuted even to the most grievous deaths. Let us set before our eyes the holy apostles. Peter, by unjust envy, underwent, not one or two, but many sufferings; till at last, being martyred, he went to the place of glory that was due unto him. For the same cause did Paul, in like manner, receive the reward of his patience. Seven times he was in bonds; he was whipped, was stoned; he preached both in the east and in the west, leaving behind him the glorious report of his faith; . . . he at last suffered martyrdom by the command of the governors. . . . To these holy apostles were joined a very great number of others, who, having through envy undergone, in like manner, many pains and torments, have left a glorious example to us. For this, not only men, but women, have been persecuted, and, having suffered very grievous and cruel punishments, have finished the course of their faith with firmness."

Passing over the testimony of intermediate writers, we present an extract from a letter of the church of Smyrna, soon after the martyrdom of Polycarp, the disciple of John, A. D. 166. Besides describing his constancy, they say, "The sufferings of all the other martyrs were blessed and generous, which they underwent according to the will of God. . . . And indeed, who can choose but admire the greatness of their minds, and that admirable patience and love of their Master which then appeared in them? who, when they were so flayed with whipping that the frame and structure of their bodies were laid open to their very inward veins and arteries, nevertheless endured it. In like manner those who were condemned to the beasts, and kept a long time in prison, underwent many cruel torments, being forced to lie upon sharp spikes laid under their bodies, and tormented with divers other sorts of punishments; that so, if it were possible, the tyrant, by the length of their sufferings, might have brought them to deny Christ."

In addition to these testimonies from earlier ages, we have that of numerous writers, both heathen and Christian, establishing the fact that at different periods during the first three centuries, the most violent persecutions raged against the Christians. These were sometimes outbreaks of popular fury, or confined to single provinces; but frequently they were carried on throughout the empire with all the resources of absolute power, and all the rage that might mark the death-struggle of the reigning superstition. Ten such general persecutions have been enumerated, and the victims have been computed at not less than three millions.

A very striking confirmation of these historical statements is found in the ancient Christian monuments existing in the catacombs at Rome. These are vast subterranean excavations, which were used by the Christians as places of burial for their dead. Their extent is such that they have been estimated to contain nearly seven millions of graves, fully confirming the accounts of ancient writers respecting the great number who embraced Christianity. Among the inscriptions here, the word Martyr, and the palm and other emblems of martyrdom, are of frequent occurrence; and in some instances the tale of Christian endurance is more fully related. (See Rawlinson's Bampton Lectures, pp. 282–288, 530.)

The later of these victims could not, of course, present in their sufferings such strong confirmation of the truth as the first had done; for their belief was founded, not on personal knowledge, but on the evidence of others. But they proved their own strong reliance on the good faith of their instructors, respecting whom they had the best means of knowledge; and these instructors, in turn, testified to the fidelity of those who went before them. The martyrs showed, too, in a most striking manner, the power of their religion to support the soul, and to impart the holiest feelings of submission to God, and of forgiveness and love to man. The prayer of the Savior, pardoning his murderers, found repeated imitation among those who suffered as his disciples. The patience and piety with which the Christians bore their persecutions, won constantly new followers, as those around saw, by such indications, the divine glory of the faith by which they were upheld.

Section 34. Conclusion.

We have thus presented, in a brief outline, the arguments for the truth of the Christian system. Much learning and ability have been employed, in times past and in our own, in developing the various portions of this evidence, and guarding the religion of Jesus, at all points, against the assaults of infidelity. Such labor has been of high importance; and yet it is not by ingenious arguments that the disciples of Christ have generally been won or secured. It has been by the beauty and holiness of the system, by its adaptation to human nature, and by the power and excellence of the influence it has been seen to exert. We conclude, therefore, with a few words upon a subject already presented among others — the Efficacy of Christianity.

This has been proved, in the first place, by the public improvements which the gospel has brought about. That it has not done all that might be desired, is confessed. It has not removed sin nor sorrow from the earth; and while man continues a free agent, no means, however powerful, can effect this. But the gospel has done much. It put an end to the cruel games of the Roman amphitheatre, where men were made to slaughter each other for the amusement of the citizens. It restrained licentiousness, and banished almost from human knowledge some forms of sensuality once freely indulged in. It has softened the conduct of war, established bounds to despotic authority, abolished the cruel and licentious form of slavery which prevailed eighteen hundred years ago, triumphed over the slavery of the feudal system, and is now exterminating, throughout the earth, that later form of this evil which till recently prevailed in our own country. It has established hospitals, and encouraged schools and universities. The greatest and best of reformers have been made such by the Christian religion. The noblest names among the benefactors of humanity are inscribed in its annals.

In more private life, the efficacy of Christianity is witnessed wherever we turn our sight. If we inquire by what power the evil propensities of a neighborhood have been subdued, we find that it was by the coming among them of some religious teacher. If we hear of a man, formerly reckless and dissolute, brought to a peaceable and sober life, we learn that he has been converted at a camp-meeting, or in some more gradual manner been brought to the love of Christ and his gospel. If we ask the bereaved what has brought them comfort, they answer, the religion of Christ. If we look around, to see what now is civilizing the globe, we find it is the gospel in the hands of Christian missionaries.

If we look within, and strive to discern with what power or influence our best thoughts and feelings are connected; by what we have been kept back from wrong or encouraged to right doing; by what we have been led to repentance, cheered in sorrow, or strengthened for virtuous effort, — we find that, from whatever the impulse directly proceeded, it was connected, nearly or remotely, with the precepts and example of Jesus Christ. The enlightening and healing power of the gospel has come to us from the guidance of Christian parents, from the teachings of the Christian pulpit, from the institutions, the customs, the habits of thought and feeling of a Christian community. We recognize in the gospel the source of every hallowed influence; we perceive its result within ourselves, and we know that the medicine must be genuine from its power to heal.

To him in whose inward experience it is fully realized, this evidence to the truth of Christianity from personal knowledge of its worth is the most powerful of all. It is this which retains, in firm allegiance to Christ, thousands who have never had it in their power to examine the testimony of antiquity, or to follow the researches of science. They know the truth of the religion because it has been to them individually "the power of God unto salvation." Let the assurance they give us encourage our efforts, and if convinced by the evidences we have surveyed, that Jesus spake the words of God, let us strive, by obedience to his holy law, to crown our speculative faith in his gospel by personal experience of its inestimable value.

QUESTIONS FOR EXAMINATION.

Section I.—1. Whence is knowledge on religious subjects commonly derived? 2. What original sources can be named? 3. What do we learn from innate ideas? 4. What from nature? 5. Why are not these means of knowledge sufficient. 6. Into what errors have men fallen with regard to the nature of God? 7. What is said of morality among the ancient heathen? 8. What of customs of society? 9. Human sacrifices? 10. Divine honors? 11. What is said of those who now reject Christianity? 12. What then seems probable? 13. What instances of God's goodness confirm this probability? 14. Of what can revelation alone assure us? 15. By what is this probability further confirmed?

Section II.—1. What is a miracle? 2. What must revelation be, and why? 3. What is implied in denying the possibility of miracle? 4. What is said of the uniformity of the laws of nature? 5. What of the power of God? 6. Why does religion appear worthy of miraculous intervention? 7. To what miracle or miracles does science testify? 8. What does Geology teach? 9. Why must the beginnings of vegetable and animal life have been miraculous? 10. How is this conclusion affected, if we admit the theory of gradual development? 11. How, if creation be resolved into a single impulse? 12. What inference can we draw from creation to revelation? 13. How may miracles be consistent with laws of nature? 14. Give the illustration of the bird in the forest. 15. That of the sunrise and the comet. 16. What has been argued from human experience? 17. To what does our individual experience amount? 18. Is all the testimony of past ages on one side? 19. On which side is the positive testimony—for miracles, or against them? 20. To what two purposes are miracles applied? 21. Why not to others? 22. What must miracles be, in order to command belief? 23. What must the revelation be which they sustain? 24. How must they be proved? 25. What does Christianity claim? 26. What passages are referred to? (This question may be asked in all future references to passages of Scripture.) 27. What does consistency require of us? 28. Supposing Christianity received on other grounds, what connection would miracles have with its authority? 29. How would they prove God's love to man? 30. What is the most suitable question for us to ask?

Section III.—1. What inquiry now meets us? 2. What is said of Christianity and civilization? 3. Of the condition of woman? 4. Character of Christians? 5. Admissions of sceptics? 6. Endeavors to improve

Christianity? 7. What idea does Christianity give of God? 8. What of man? 9. Of duty? 10. Of man's destiny? 11. For what does it alone exhibit a fitness? 12. What is said of the requirements of Mohammedanism? 13. Of Judaism? 14. How does Christianity differ from them? 15. From what does it propose to save its disciples?

Section IV. — 1. What are the other religions in the world? 2. How was Judaism given? 3. In what respects is it incomplete? 4. How is the spirit of Judaism, in some former ages, exemplified in the second book of Esdras? 5. From what is Mohammedanism derived? 6. What is its character? 7. What is said of Mormonism? 8. Why may Buddhism be distinguished from other heathen religions? 9. What are some of its characteristics? 10. What is said of Heathenism? 11. What is said of ancient philosophers? 12. Of Plato? 13. What is said of other religions respecting miracles? 14. What of Mohammedanism? 15. Brahminism and Heathenism? 16. By what names is Deism sometimes called? 17. From what are its doctrines in great part derived? 18. What doctrines are doubted by some among those who reject Christianity?

Section V. — 1. In what does Christianity coincide with natural religion? 2. How has modern science made this clearer? 3. What resemblance between God's government in nature and in Christianity with regard to small things? 4. What in regard to the practical and the theoretical? 5. How does Christianity teach concerning a future life? 6. How does Mohammedanism? 7. How is Christianity analogous to nature in its operation on the heart, and on society? 8. How in its remedial character? 9. How in its mediatorial character? 10. What cases of suffering are analogous to the death of Christ? 11. How has this agreement with nature been used as an argument against Christianity? 12. Why should we not expect all the teachings of Jesus to be new? 13. For what purposes, beyond the teaching of new truth, did he come?

Section VI. — 1. How otherwise may the harmony of Christianity with nature be seen? 2. How is it addressed to the intellect? 3. How to the imagination? 4. Give an account of some of the passages referred to. 5. How is Christianity adapted to the conscience and the will? 6. What is said respecting future judgment? 7. What of the excitement of conscience? 8. Hope of pardon and assistance? 9. How is it adapted to the affections in the idea it presents of God? 10. How in that of the Savior? 11. How in regard to the domestic and social affections? (Under each question give the passages referred to.)

Section VII. — 1. What does the moral law of Christianity embrace? 2. How are these principles taught by heathen philosophers, by the Old Testament, and by Christ? 3. What further rules are given by Christianity, expressly or by implication? 4. In what respects is Christianity a system of restraint? 5. What opposite evil does it avoid? 6. What virtues have been most popular? 7. What least so? 8. Which would an uninspired teacher have chiefly commended, and why? 9. Why would an ambitious leader have urged them? 10. Which did Jesus commend? 11. How do his precepts of meekness and forgiveness appear practicable? 12. What did this course show? 13. Did he discountenance then the popular class of virtues? 14. Why did he not directly commend them? 15. How did he encourage them? 16. Give the passages referred to. 17. To what does Christianity ascribe the evils that exist? 18. How have reformers in general directed their efforts? 19. Why have they done right in this? 20. Why, then, has Christianity done better? 21. Why would not a fanatic have taken this ground? 22. An impostor? 23. How have some defended certain evil institutions? 24. How has the same fact been used by others? 25. What furnishes a reply to both arguments? 26. What is said of despotism? 27. What of the gladiatorial combats? 28. What principles did Christ lay down? 29. What institutions and practices are condemned by him? 30. What distinction may be made by objectors between receiving the morality of Christ and receiving his religion? 31. If one sincerely obeys his moral precepts, what will probably follow? 32. What does the holiness of the system prove? 33. With what is its morality inseparably connected? 34. Give the substance of the extract from Professor Norton.

Section VIII. — 1. What is said of the personal character of the founder, in most systems? 2. What claim did Jesus make? 3. Why would not a fanatic have done thus? 4. Why would not an impostor? 5. What has been admitted by many, who did not receive Christianity as divinely revealed? 6. What are the words of Rousseau? 7. What those of Rénan? 8. What qualities does the Savior's character combine? 9. What text illustrates his feelings as a citizen? 10. What as a friend? 11. What as a son? 12. What his courage and gentleness? 13. What his superiority to prejudice, and his wise self-control? 14. What his regard for the law, while he blamed the Pharisees? 15. What his course respecting the distribution of property? 16. What his dignity and meekness? 17. The manner in which he called his followers to him? 18. When does the beauty of his character most appear? 19. What are the instances referred to as preceding his crucifixion? 20. Those accompanying his crucifixion? 21. What is one of the highest achievements of art? 22. What is inferred from this? 23. Can you name any of the incidents here mentioned which the writers could be supposed to have derived from previous narratives? 24. What is said of the prayer for his murderers? 25. What of his words to the penitent thief? 26. Give the substance of the passage from President Hill.

Section IX. — 1. From what source may another argument for Christianity be derived? 2. What is said of the change produced eighteen centuries since? 3. Of the teacher who wrought this change? 4. How may so great a result, from means apparently so inadequate, be regarded? 5. What is said of the birth of Jesus? 6. Of his education? 7. Of his means of support? 8. Of the opposition against him? 9. Of the greatness of his claims? 10. What power did he claim? 11. What in regard to his conduct? 12. What titles and rank in connection with the Jewish nation? 13. What connection with God? 14. What did he foretell respecting himself? 15. By what other lofty titles did he announce himself? 16. How must he be regarded, if not divinely commissioned? 17. In what manner did he make these claims? 18. What plan did he connect with them? 19. What fate did he foretell for himself? 20. How did this knowledge affect him? 21. Why can we not regard him as deluded? 22. Why not as an impostor? 23. What is said of the course he pursued? 24. What sects existed among the Jews at that time? 25. What did Jesus denounce in the Pharisees? 26. In what did he differ from the Sadducees? 27. In what from the Essenes? 28. What feeling had they all in common? 29. How would a fanatic have done? 30. How an impostor? 31. How did Jesus? 32. How respecting ceremonies? 33. Respecting the Samaritans? 34. Respecting the Temple? 35. What course did he pursue with regard to the Gentiles? 36. Yet what was the result? 37. What is said of the first day's preaching? 38. Effect of persecution? 39. Contest with Roman power? 40. With barbarism? 41. Of the present prospects of Christianity? 42. How is this triumphant system considered by modern sceptics?

Section X. — 1. For what reason, besides direct evidence, do the death and resurrection of Jesus claim our belief? 2. What is said of some of the facts of Christianity? 3. What are these? 4. What is the tradition of the church respecting the death of the Savior? 5. What is that of its opponents? 6. What does a reformer incur? 7. How if he claims a divine commission? 8. What, then, is it agreed, did Jesus undergo? 9. What is said of crucifixion? 10. What must have been the state of his followers after his death? 11. If they had remained in this condition, could the religion have prevailed? 12. What restored their faith and courage, according to their own account? 13. How was the resurrection of Jesus proclaimed? 14. What is the testimony of the book of Acts? 15. What that of 1 Corinthians? 16. What is the admission of Strauss? 17. If Jesus did not rise from the dead, what must one of his followers have been? 18. What, in that case, did this disciple accomplish? 19. How does modern scepticism meet this argument? 20. What have some fancied? 21. What does this fail to explain? 22. Why? 23. What is the theory of Strauss on this subject? 24. How only would such an illusion be possible? 25. In what, then, does this explanation fail? 26. How does Strauss account for the testimony of St. Paul? 27. How does this consist with the strength of the apostle's mind? 28. To what further objection is this supposition liable?

Section XI. — 1. What has been inferred from the present existence and power of Christianity? 2. What similar argument is now proposed? 3. What is said of this proof, in reference to others? 4. Of what do institutions afford proof? 5. What does the observance of the Fourth of July prove? 6. How if all records were lost? 7. Why could not the observance have arisen in intervening ages of darkness? 8. From what kind of cause must it have arisen? 9. What would decide respecting the real cause? 10. What was the Passover? 11. Is it still observed? 12. What does it commemorate? 13. Why could it not have been instituted at any intervening point of time? 14. What does the observance prove? 15. What respecting the history which records that event? 16. What does the Feast of Tabernacles prove? 17. What the Feast of Purim? 18. What other Jewish institutions? 19. What are named as New Testament institutions? 20. Describe the Communion. 21. Why could not this have been introduced in any intervening age? 22. From what age must it have come down? 23. What do the words connected with it imply, as to the author of the custom? 24. What must he have foreseen? 25. Why must his anticipation have been accomplished? 26. What might he have done? 27. How does this appear? 28. What did he do instead? 29. What qualities does this rite show that he possessed? 30. What respecting the fulfilment of his expectations for the success of his cause? 31. What, then, does the ordinance prove with regard to the character and endowments of the Savior? (It may be interesting and useful to follow out, in a similar manner, the argument to be derived from the ordinance of Baptism, Matt. xxviii. 19; that from the institution of the ministry, Matt. x. 1; 2 Tim. ii. 2; and that from "the Lord's Day," John xx. 19, 26; Acts xx. 7; 1 Cor. xvi. 2; Rev. i. 10.)

Section XII. — 1. What claim is peculiar to the religion of the Bible? 2. What was the character of the age in which Jesus lived? 3. By whom were his actions, instructions, and miracles witnessed and recorded? 4. At what risk were the statements of these witnesses made? 5. By whom were they received as true? 6. What of contradictory accounts? 7. What of legendary additions? 8. What are the records of Christianity? 9. When is a book genuine? 10. When is it authentic? 11. Into what classes is the evidence divided? 12. What traditional evidence have we for the books of the New Testament? 13. What is said of the original manuscripts? 14. How many manuscripts of the Gospels have been examined? 15. What is the age of some of them? 16. What is said of the manuscripts of ancient versions? 17. What of the works of the Christian Fathers? 18. When are the Gospels admitted to have been in common use? 19. What is the era of the ascendency of Christianity? 20. By what event was this marked? 21. What did the Roman empire then comprise? 22. Who wrote about this time? 23. What testimony does he give to the books of the New Testament? 24. Of what does he speak doubtfully? 25. Of what does he speak as undoubtedly genuine? 26. What does this discrimination show? 27. When did Origen die? 28. How early was he engaged in expounding the Scriptures? 29. What does he testify respecting the Gospels? 30. What is said of his quotations? 31. What was the period of Tertullian? 32. What is said of the quotations in this writer? 33. When did Clement of Alexandria flourish? 34. Of what does he give an account? 35. What distinction does he make? 36. What is the Muratorian Canon? 37. What is its date? 38. How is this ascertained? 39. Of what books does it speak as canonical? 40. By whom and when was it discovered?

Section XIII. — 1. When did Irenæus live? 2. Where and from whom did he receive instruction? 3. Where did he afterwards minister? 4. How do these facts affect the value of his evidence? 5. What account does he give of the origin of the Gospels? 6. What letter was written about A. D. 170? 7. To what books does it contain references? 8. What was then the age of Pothinus, bishop of Lyons? 9. What do these facts indicate? 10. When did Justin live, and why is he called Martyr? 11. What is said of his quotations? 12. What account does he give of the Savior? 13. How far does this differ from the Gospels? 14. In what instances does he refer to the Gospel of John? 15. Why are these quotations of especial importance? 16. How has this evidence been met? 17. How is the objection removed by the recently discovered Sinaitic manuscript? 18. What is the date of Papias? 19. By whom is a fragment of his writing preserved? 20. What is his testimony? 21. With whose does it agree? 22. Where did Polycarp preside? 23. When and how did he die? 24. What was his answer when life was offered him if he would revile Christ? 25. Of whom had he been a scholar? 26. What does Irenæus record of him? 27. What allusions does his Epistle contain? 28. In what books are the passages alluded to? 29. By whom and where is Clement of Rome named? 30. From what Gospel does Clement quote? 31. From what Epistles? 32. Who are generally called the Apostolical Fathers, and why? 33. Whom does Papias quote as his instructor? 34. Who does "John the Elder" appear to have been, from the testimony of Irenæus? 35. What has been conjectured of the Gospels used by some of these Fathers? 36. What appears from Luke i. 1. 37. Why did these other writings disappear? 38. What would have been the case if they had contained different accounts? 39. What shows that they were the same with ours? 40. What is said finally of the testimony of Papias?

Section XIV. — 1. What fact strengthens the testimony of the Fathers? 2. How is this instanced in Eusebius? (See p. 40.) 3. When did Dionysius live, and respecting what book did he express doubt? 4. Origen? 5. Caius? 6. What do these facts prove? 7. What has been the general decision since respecting the books then doubted? 8. What ought our decision to be respecting those which were then undoubted? 9. From what else can we infer the truth of the Gospels? 10. What passages show the prominence given to events in the history of Jesus? 11. What is remarked by Mr. Norton? 12. To what class do the writers thus far quoted belong? 13. What other class was there? 14. Who were the earliest of these? 15. What were the Ebionites, and their views? 16. What is said of the Gospel they possessed? 17. What other class of heretics was there? 18. From what source were their ideas derived? 19. What does their name imply? 20. How do they seem to have formed their systems? 21. How were they disposed with regard to anything Jewish? 22. About what time did Marcion live? 23. What was his course with regard to the Gospels? 24. What did Heracleon write, and when? 25. What is said of Valentinus in relation to John's Gospel? 26. The Montanists? 27. The Alogi? 28. When did Basilides live, and what did he write? 29. With what Gospels was he acquainted? 30. Had the early Gnostics any other Gospels than ours? 31. What is said of other books called Gospels among the later Gnostics? 32. What does Tertullian assert? 33. How does he argue against their right to do this? 34. What does this argument prove? 35. What is said by Paley respecting early sects?

Section XV. — 1. To what class of writers do we now turn? 2. When were the Talmuds composed? 3. Of what particulars connected with Christianity do they speak? 4. What account do they give of the miracles of Christ? 5. Why is their testimony valuable? 6. Who was Josephus? 7. What direct references to Christ appear in his works? 8. What is said of these passages? 9. In what is his evidence of most value? 10. Exemplify this in his account of Herod I. 11. Of Herod Antipas. 12. Agrippa I. 13. Agrippa II. 14. What heathen writers are named? 15. Who was Julian? 16. What is said of his testimony? 17. When did Porphyry write? 18. What is said of his work? 19. To what Christian writings did he refer? 20. Who was Celsus? 21. From what source do we learn respecting his book? 22. What words did he use? 23. What is remarked respecting them? 24. Of what does he accuse the Christians? 25. From what did the various readings probably result? 26. What do they prove? 27. What other expression of Celsus proves the antiquity of the Christian writings? 28. What are the particulars to which Celsus refers by way of objection? 29. What does his language prove? 30. How long was this after the earliest of the Gospels claims to have been written? 31. To what conclusion does this lead us? 32. From what other source is evidence derived? 33. When was the ancient Syriac version made? 34. What do the versions confirm? 35. What does their existence show? 36. From what other writings may a similar argument be drawn? 37. What other source of evidence is mentioned? 38. What is said of a coin of Cyprus? 39. Of Philippi? 40. Of coins of Ephesus?

Section XVI.—1. What is the Internal Evidence? 2. What is said of the language? 3. What examples of Hebraisms in the use of "and"? 4. "Lo," or "behold"? 5. "Answered"? 6. In a proverbial expression? 7. In the expression "New Birth"? 8. What of the acquaintance of the New Testament writers with certain subjects? 9. How is it with such accuracy in fictitious writing? 10. What chapter is taken as an example? 11. What is said of the position of the three provinces? 12. The name of a city? 13. The parcel of ground? 14. The mountain? 15. The Samaritan worship? 16. Jealousy of Jews and Samaritans? 17. What passages in Scripture agree with these representations? 18. What existing facts confirm them? 19. What is the testimony of Rénan? 20. Of Strauss? 21. In what besides geography is this accuracy perceived? 22. How is this exemplified in the Herod family? 23. What makes these facts of more importance? 24. Where did the Gospel find its most numerous adherents? 25. What took place after the Jewish war? 26. What is said of books from Jewish Christian writers after that time? 27. How is the argument briefly expressed?

Section XVII.—1. What is the third point in the Internal Evidences? 2. What is said of eulogy and personal description? 3. Exceptions to this remark? 4. What of unfavorable incidents? 5. The Savior's trial? 6. Mention of doubts? 7. What is the fourth point spoken of? 8. How illustrated in the disciples' conduct? 9. How by words in the language spoken by Jesus? 10. How is the use of these words accounted for? 11. What is the fifth point spoken of? 12. In what character, and how, is this exemplified? 13. What is the sixth point referred to? 14. By what is Mark characterized? 15. What is said of Matthew and Luke in their accounts of Christ's birth? 16. What is said of the Sermon on the Mount? 17. What parables and incidents are given by Luke alone? 18. What occurrences does John alone relate? 19. How does his manner of relating parables differ from the others? 20. What is said of his style? 21. What examples respecting the dignity of the Savior? 22. What of spiritual grandeur? 23. How do the narratives agree? 24. What is said of differences in thought and language? 25. What of differences in the narrative? 26. By what historical event is this illustrated?

Section XVIII.—1. What is the seventh point mentioned? 2. Exemplify this in connection with the Last Supper. 3. What is the case sometimes, when accounts are apparently contradictory? 4. How is this exemplified? 5. What was the charge against Jesus, as related by Luke? 6. The reply of Pilate? 7. Why does this reply seem strange? 8. What is the explanation, and where found? 9. What is omitted by John? 10. How supplied by Luke? 11. What is said of coincidences among the first three Gospels? 12. What have some inferred from this? 13. What name is given by these writers to the first three Evangelists? 14. What is probable, respecting the original Gospel, had it existed? 15. What is the fact? 16. What is, probably, the true explanation? 17. What must have been current in the primitive churches, and therefore the true basis of all the Gospels? 18. What is the eighth point mentioned? 19. What is said of the genuineness of the Epistles? 20. Why could they not possibly have been forgeries? 21. To what subjects do they relate? 22. How do they agree with the Gospels and Acts regarding the resurrection of Christ? 23. Where is the account of the Lord's Supper confirmed? 24. How is the character of Peter illustrated?

Section XIX. — 1. Among what books is the agreement most strikingly discernible? 2. How is the authority of the Acts and the Epistles established? 3. In what work is this proof developed? 4. Exemplify the agreement of the accounts in Paul's first visit to Jerusalem. 5. In regard to his visit to Athens, in what do the accounts agree? 6. In what do they differ? 7. How is the difference accounted for? 8. What of the preaching of Apollos at Corinth? 9. What do we learn from Romans of Paul's contemplated visit to Jerusalem? 10. What from Acts of the same visit? 11. How do we learn that the historian was a companion of Paul? 12. What do we learn from the conclusion of the Acts? 13. How does it appear that the Gospel of Luke and the Acts were by the same author? 14. When was Luke's Gospel written, and how does this appear? 15. What does this chain of evidence prove respecting the authorship of this Gospel? 16. What respecting its date, with reference to the crucifixion?

Section XX. — 1. To what other writings may a similar train of argument be applied? 2. What does the writer of the fourth Gospel claim? 3. How is this claim affected if the verse which contains it is from another hand? 4. What is said of his style? 5. Where do we learn the name of the writer? 6. What may be conjectured from the remark in John xxi. 23? 7. What from the circumlocutions by which he conceals his name? 8. What is said of the prominence given to this apostle? 9. How does Rénan account for this? 10. How would such weakness affect his character as an historian? 11. What is the more probable explanation? 12. What other supposition remains? 13. If this were true, what would the Gospel still be to us? 14. Why is this theory less probable? 15. By what writers has the genuineness of this Gospel been especially attacked? 16. What are the arguments brought against it? 17. How do we reply to that from the difference of its narrative? 18. In what respects is John's Gospel supplementary? 19. How did his personal attachment affect his writing? 20. How his spiritual insight? 21. What is said, however, of the testimony of the other evangelists to the same objects? 22. Why do these critics consider the idea of the Logos as indicating a later date? 23. In what early writer does the same idea occur? 24. What is said of its occurrence in the Apocalypse? (Rev. xix. 13.) 25. How is the fact accounted for that the other Gospels do not mention the raising of Lazarus? 26. What other explanation is suggested? 27. How is the apparent difference with regard to the Last Supper explained? 28. How is the "moral miracle" of Christianity affected if the fourth Gospel is set aside? 29. If the transactions it records did not take place, what must have been the endowments of its inventor? 30. How do these endowments render it improbable that he should impose a false Gospel on the world? 31. That he should leave no trace of his existence except a forgery? 32. What is the admission of Rénan?

Section XXI. — 1. What endeavor has been made to depreciate the authentic Gospels? 2. What are the Apocrypha of the New Testament? 3. What result is here anticipated from their examination? 4. What may be inferred from Luke's preface? 5. Why did these accounts fall into disuse? 6. Which seems to have been the most important of them? 7. With what may it have been identical? 8. By whom is it quoted? 9. What other Gospel is mentioned? 10. By whom is it mentioned? 11. What was his knowledge of it? 12. What further is said of these books? 13. What is the assertion of Paley?

14. What is said of the date of the Apocrypha of the New Testament? 15. How do they compare with the authentic Gospels? 16. Who is quoted as authority in the First Gospel of the Infancy? 17. How does this agree with what we know of Jewish High Priests, and of Caiaphas in particular? 18. What wonder is he said to relate? 19. What titles are given to Mary in the same Gospel? 20. What is the story of the boy possessed with devils? 21. The cures wrought by the Virgin with water? 22. Transformation of the young man? 23. Miracle of the throne? 24. Fate of the boy who ran against Jesus? 25. Complaint of the parents, and subsequent conduct ascribed to Jesus? 26. What account is given of Carinus and Leucius? 27. What is told of Pilate? 28. Acknowledgment of the Jewish Council? 29. Prophecy they are said to have discovered? 30. Subsequent action and fate of Pilate? 31. What remarks are made upon the character of these stories? 32. From what did they probably originate? 33. Which of these documents purports to be from the hand of Jesus himself? 34. How may the "Gospel of Nicodemus" be regarded? 35. How far are the apocryphal writings inconsistent with the genuine Gospels?

Section XXII. — 1. What appears to be now established respecting the Gospels? 2. What of other books? 3. For what would this be sufficient? 4. How exemplified in the fourth Gospel? 5. What else, however, is proved? 6. What proofs are especially referred to? 7. What is said of the general voice of antiquity? 8. Its unanimity? 9. How exemplified? 10. Number of the witnesses? 11. What objection from disagreement of copies? 12. What is said of the number of various readings? 13. What of their importance? 14. How are they accounted for? 15. What is said of the claims of these records? 16. How illustrated in a modern instance? 17. On what account are they objected to? 18. By whom is this position taken? 19. How have they been led to it? 20. What have scientific researches produced? 21. Why has this conviction been considered opposed to miracle? 22. How is the objection answered? 23. What is said of intellectual philosophy for a century past? 24. What system has prevailed in Germany? 25. By what names illustrated? 26. What is one distinguishing trait of it? 27. How far is this commendable? 28. When is it carried to an extreme? 29. What is assumed by some recent writers? 30. What does this assumption show? 31. What is the remark of Strauss? 32. Against what does Rénan protest? 33. Still, what conclusion does he reach, previous to examination?

Section XXIII. — 1. Of what is a view proposed to be given? 2. On what supposition does the first class of these theories proceed? 3. What is to be classed among these? 4. What author has attempted this? 5. To what does he ascribe many of the Gospel wonders? 6. To what remarkable miracle is this view applied? 7. In what manner? 8. To what miracles, among others, is this theory inapplicable? 9. Where it is used, to what objection is it liable? 10. How is the passage, John ix. 32, applied to this theory? 11. What is said of the manner in which it has been advocated? 12. What is the representation of the German Naturalists? 13. Who is the best known among them? 14. How does Dr. Paulus explain the miracle of the fish and the piece of money? 15. How the raising of Lazarus? 16. How the ascension? 17. What opinion of previous writers does Strauss perceive implied in this theory of Paulus? 18. What was the fancy of Bahrdt? 19. That of Brennecke? 20. That of

Paulus with regard to the fate of Jesus? 21. What opinion does Strauss express respecting them? 22. What is said of the conduct ascribed to Jesus by these theories?

Section XXIV. — 1. What is the second class of theories? 2. How does Rénan conceive Jesus to have assumed the position of wonder-worker? 3. How would this explanation affect our estimate of him? 4. In what instance does Rénan suppose Jesus to have been himself deceived? 5. By whom, and for what purpose? 6. What event has been the subject of the boldest speculations? 7. For what reason was this? 8. On what two ideas do the explanations proceed? 9. How is the death of Jesus explained by some? 10. What is urged in support of this? 11. What cases referred to? 12. How were these persons restored? 13. What would be required, then, to explain the restoration of Jesus? 14. What is the supposition of Bahrdt as to the plan of Jesus? 15. As to the agents in his restoration? 16. What have others ascribed to his disciples? 17. What did Schuster suppose? 18. What is the theory of a writer in the Westminster Review? 19. What orders is Pilate supposed to have given, and why? 20. What is observed respecting the thrust with a spear? 21. What respecting the slowness of recovery in such a case? 22. Why cannot we believe that Jesus was mistaken in thinking he had been dead? 23. Why not that he was deceiving his disciples? 24. To what does Rénan ascribe the story of the resurrection? 25. What objection is made to this theory?

Section XXV. — 1. What is the ground taken by many? 2. Why cannot this be held consistently? 3. How is this exemplified in the account of the raising of Lazarus? 4. What is said of the portions being interwoven? 5. How exemplified in the same account? 6. What name is given to the theory of Dr. Strauss? 7. How far is it peculiarly his? 8. How does it suppose the stories respecting Jesus to have arisen? 9. With what purpose did the evangelists collect these myths? 10. How are the miraculous incidents considered? 11. How those not miraculous? 12. What remains as true respecting Jesus? 13. With what is this theory inconsistent? 14. How does the Christian era differ from the ages of fable? 15. What is said of the periods allowed by Strauss for the production of myths? 16. How would Jewish myths have represented the Messiah? 17. What do the Apocrypha of the New Testament show us? 18. Why cannot we believe that the myths originated from the companions of Jesus? 19. Why not, that they left no authentic account? 20. Had they left such, could the mythical account have superseded it? 21. What would have been the interest of the enemies of Jesus? 22. What does their explanation of his miracles imply? 23. What would have prevented the reception of these myths by the Gentile Christians? 24. What is the Christian religion, apart from the question of its divine origin? 25. From what did it arise, according to this theory? 26. What is said of a later work of Dr. Strauss? 27. What does he here represent to be the date of the Gospels? 28. What respecting intentional fiction? 29. How does he regard Jesus? 30. What is said of the legendary history of Greece and Rome? 31. What of the history of our Lord? 32. With what miracle is the narrative crowned? 33. With what supposition is the mythical theory finally compared?

Section XXVI. — 1. Why is the Old Testament of value to us? 2. How is it sustained by quotations in the New? 3. How by the position of the

Savior? 4. How does the Old Testament sustain the New by prophecies? 5. By what peculiarities of its character? 6. What system does the Old Testament present? 7. How does this appear from its first principle? 8. How in contrast with Egyptian superstition? 9. How by the name it gives to the Supreme? 10. How by representations of his nature? 11. How by his moral attributes, and his power, wisdom, and providence? 12. How by the Ten Commandments? 13. How by laws relating to the poor? 14. How by treatment of defective institutions? 15. How by contrast with idolatry? 16. How by passages of especial sublimity and beauty? 17. Give an account of the 23d psalm. (The same of each of the other passages referred to.)

Section XXVII. — 1. Why are ancient documents liable to be obscure? 2. What was customary with ancient writers? 3. What passages will this fact explain? 4. On what authority do some of the narratives rest? 5. How far is the compiler of Genesis accountable for what is there related? 6. From what source is Joshua x. 12–14 derived? 7. What is observed with regard to errors in matters of science? 8. Censurable conduct of persons who are mentioned with approval? 9. Standard of morals, and peculiar temptations? 10. Supposed incorrect sentiments of the sacred historian? 11. Doubts regarding any particular books? 12. What facts would remain undisturbed? 13. What result sometimes appears from free investigation? 14. What disposition appears in some writers? 15. What passages, among others, contradict such representations? 16. What is said of the sacrifice of Isaac? 17. What is Mr. Parker's tribute to the Hebrew system?

Section XXVIII. — 1. By what kinds of evidence is the Old Testament sustained? 2. Of external evidence, what is the testimony of the Jewish nation? 3. What is said of the care with which the books have been preserved? 4. What do the Christian Scriptures prove, if regarded merely as ancient works? 5. What is said of Josephus? 6. What of Philo? 7. What of the Apocryphal books? 8. The Samaritans? 9. What of the Samaritan Pentateuch? 10. What renders their testimony the more valuable? 11. What other sources of evidence are mentioned? 12. Name some of the heathen writers who ascribe the Jewish laws to Moses? 13. When did Hecatæus and Manetho live? 14. What of Longinus? 15. What ancient Hindoo poem is mentioned? 16. Give an account of the quotation from it. 17. What similar account is given, and by whom? 18. What of the records of Berosus and Manetho? 19. What is related by Moses of Chorene and others? 20. Who was Nicolaus, and what testimony does he give? 21. How is the marriage of Ahab illustrated? 22. What particulars in regard to Eithobalus agree with the characters of Jezebel and Athaliah? 23. What coincidence is there in regard to two of the later Egyptian kings? 24. By what monuments are events in sacred history illustrated? 25. Conquest of Rehoboam by Shishak? 26. Kingdoms of Israel and Judah? 27. Reign of Ben-hadad? 28. Intervention of Tiglath Pileser? 29. Altar of Ahaz? 30. Subjugation of Hezekiah? 31. Captivity of Manasseh? 32. So, or Sevech, king of Egypt? 33. Why has the account of Belshazzar appeared contrary to history? 34. How is this explained by a recent discovery? 35. In what does the internal evidence of the Old Testament consist? 36. What does the history in Exodus exhibit? 37. How is this exemplified in the passage of the Red Sea? 38. What two accounts corroborate each other? 39. What other books coincide frequently with the historical? 40. What of the argument from institutions? 41. What is the great evidence to us for the Old Testament? 42. What is said of questions of Old Testament criticism?

Section XXIX. — 1. From what is an important branch of Christian evidence derived? 2. What is said of the history of the Jews? 3. Belief of other nations regarding the golden age? 4. What of the Hebrew view? 5. What anticipation appears through the Jewish history? 6. What of this anticipation at the Christian era? 7. From what writers do we learn this? 8. What of this expectation among the Jews since that time? 9. In what character did the Jews expect the Messiah to appear? 10. What is said of passages inconsistent with this idea? 11. What did some Jewish writers assert? 12. What took place at the period when this expectation was strongest? 13. From whom is Jesus represented as descended? 14. What did he call the community he established? 15. How was the term justified? 16. How of the predictions of suffering? 17. What objections are brought against this being regarded as the fulfilment of the national expectation? 18. What is essential to the character of prophecy? 19. What were the reasons for the rejection of Jesus? 20. What answer had the Jews to the evidence of miracles? 21. How does the chief reason of the Jews for rejecting Jesus appear to us? 22. How does the station which they expected him to assume compare with his real one? 23. In what question did he suggest this thought? 24. What is said of an uninspired Jew entertaining this idea? 25. What rejection and choice would it imply? 26. What would be the probability of his thus succeeding? 27. In what station would the prophets naturally expect the Messiah to appear? 28. What appears, from some indications in the prophets, with regard to their predictions? 29. What might have taken place if the Jews had accepted Jesus? 30. Why is the above argument independent of particular prophecies? 31. State briefly what the argument is.

Section XXX. — 1. What claims does the Jewish religion possess? 2. State some of the grounds of these claims. 3. What is there in contrast with these claims? 4. In what respects does it show its national character? 5. Its purpose to keep the people apart from other nations? 6. If the Jewish laws were of later date than Moses, what must still be true of them? 7. If the account of the deliverance from Egypt were of later date, what must still be true respecting it? 8. For what reason? 9. What suppositions may be formed to account for the Jewish religion? 10. What does the first supposition imply? 11. What respecting those who taught it? 12. Why cannot this be believed? 13. What contrast is pointed out between the Jewish nation and others, and what inference drawn? 14. With what is the second supposition inconsistent? 15. In what respects? 16. What of the brotherhood of mankind? 17. What of the divine unity and care for all mankind? 18. What do these limitations show? 19. What fulfils this promise? 20. How does it regard the Jewish religion? 21. What difficulty would meet us without Christianity? 22. What without Judaism? 23. What is said of the period when the new light was given? 24. What was the condition of the Jewish system? 25. What of heathen systems? 26. What of the political changes in the East? 27. Of those in the West? 28. Final ascendency of the Romans? 29. Heathen philosophy? 30. Close of the civil wars? 31. Settlement of Jews in various places? 32. What indications of divine providence do we recognize? 33. What objection is named? 34. How is this answered? 35. How is this exemplified in the existence of Jewish communities? 36. What question is suggested concerning the long delay of revelation? 37. Of what do sacred and profane history give intimations? 38. What was probably derived from this? 39. How did this early knowledge become corrupted and weakened? 40. What was sent to supply its place?

Section XXXI. — 1. Of what two descriptions are the Old Testament prophecies? 2. To what do the instances given, of the first description, relate? 3. How is the fulfilment of these evident? 4. What are such predictions respecting Nineveh? 5. Moab? 6. Philistia? 7. Edom? 8. When and how did the fulfilment of this prophecy appear? 9. Egypt? 10. Tyre? 11. Babylon? 12. What has been the disposition of some theologians? 13. What psalm is referred to in illustration? 14. What is its title? 15. Repeat some verses that are not applicable to any temporal prince. 16. What has been the usual explanation? 17. What is said of the prophetic insight into the future? 18. What was known to the prophets? 19. Under what character did they conceive of him? 20. What would they be led to hope in connection with the respective monarchs of whom they wrote? 21. What prospects would become blended in their description? 22. How is this exemplified in Ps. ii.? 23. In Ps. xlv.? 24. In Ps. lxxii.? 25. In Is. vii. 14? 26. Perhaps in Dan. ix.? 27. By what will this evidence not be materially affected? 28. Whatever the source of the prophets' foreknowledge, what will still remain? 29. What prophecy is given from Gen. xxii. 18? 30. How does this differ from the natural aspiration of a rude age? 31. What is said of the first words of Ps. xxii.? 32. Repeat the other verses quoted. 33. What renders the coincidence of verse 16 more remarkable? 34. What is the language of Ps. cx. 4? 35. How is this explained, and where, in the New Testament? 36. How is the objection answered that this psalm speaks of a conquering monarch? 37. Repeat Is. ix. 6. 38. What is said of the translation? 39. What still does the passage indicate? 40. What is said Is. xlix. 5, 6? 41. What remark is made upon it? 42. What chapter is referred to? 43. Where in the New Testament is the passage in Is. liii. referred to? 44. Repeat the 5th, 6th, and 7th verses. 45. The 8th, 9th, and 10th, in the version of Dr. Noyes. 46. Repeat Mic. v. 2. 47. Where is this referred to in the New Testament? 48. What is predicted in Hag. ii. 7, 9? 49. In Mal. iii. 1? 50. In Mal. iv. 5, 6? 51. How is this referred to in the New Testament? 52. How are the Old and New Testaments connected?

Section XXXII. — 1. What other proof is there from prophecy? 2. To what do the most remarkable of the New Testament prophecies relate? 3. Where are these found at most length? 4. Where else do they appear, in a striking form? 5. What especial marks of genuineness do these passages bear? 6. Quote the passages referred to. 7. What is said of their fulfilment? 8. Describe the Jewish rebellion, and its result. 9. What objection is named? 10. How is this answered by reference to the figurative language employed? 11. How by comparison with the ancient prophets? 12. How has the Old Testament been seen to be prophetic of the New? 13. How do the life and death of Jesus imply the overthrow of the Jewish state? 14. How long had that state existed? 15. What had it survived? 16. What was its prospect of endurance? 17. What were the character and power of the Roman dominion?

18. What treatment did Jesus and his claims receive? 19. If he was the Messiah, what did this rejection of him render necessary? 20. To what considerations was this due? 21. If the Jewish state had stood uninjured, what argument would the fact have afforded? 22. How did the rejection of Christ receive its punishment? 23. How was this event regarded when it took place? 24. With what was the overthrow of the Jewish nation in accordance? 25. What is said of their attachment to their law? 26. How only can they be considered as having incurred the threatened penalty? 27. What prophecy in Deuteronomy is referred to? 28. What reference is made to it in the New Testament? 29. What is said of the Jews since that time? 30. What is their continued existence? 31. What is said of the Romans? 32. Other Western nations of that period? 33. Of the Greeks? 34. Circumstances which threatened the destruction of the Jews? 35. Their present state? 36. What is said of predictions yet unfulfilled? 37. For what purpose, perhaps, are they preserved? 38. What are the passages referred to?

Section XXXIII. — 1. In how many aspects may the sufferings of the early Christians be regarded? 2. How do they show the truth of the accounts given? 3. How the excellence of the religion? 4. What qualities did the martyrs display? 5. Whose sufferings are first to be considered? 6. What confirms the account of these sufferings? 7. What would the enemies of Jesus have done, if possible? 8. What facts, then, are established? 9. What do these show? 10. If his claims had been false, what would have been his endeavor? 11. What effect would an evil conscience have had? 12. What is said of his last utterances, on this supposition? 13. How does such conduct compare with all we know respecting him? 14. By whose sufferings, besides those of Jesus, is Christianity confirmed? 15. In what manner? 16. How illustrated in the resurrection of Jesus? 17. What might be presumed from the nature of the case? 18. How did they offend the Jews? 19. How the Gentiles? 20. What result would probably follow? 21. What instance is mentioned in Scripture of their enduring exile? 22. Scourging? 23. Imprisonment? 24. Stoning? 25. The loss of life? 26. What martyrdom is related by Josephus? 27. When and how did this take place? 28. What words in this account are doubtful? 29. What appears, even if these words were subsequently added? 30. By what writer is the account confirmed? 31. When was Tacitus born? 32. What suspicion, does he tell us, fell upon Nero? 33. Upon whom did he charge the crime, and with what motive? 34. What account does Tacitus give of the Christians? 35. What tortures were inflicted on them? 36. What is the account of Suetonius? 37. What poets refer to the same occurrences? 38. To what torture do they particularly allude? 39. What station did Pliny hold, and when? 40. To whom did he write respecting the Christians? 41. What did he say of the spread of Christianity? 42. What punishments had Pliny inflicted? 43. What of informations? 44. What had Pliny learned of the conduct of the Christians? 45. What answer did he receive from the emperor? 46. Which of the apostles are mentioned by Clement of Rome as having suffered death? 47. Of what other sufferers does he speak? 48. From what letter is an extract given? 49. What tortures does it commemorate? 50. Through what centuries did the persecutions continue? 51. How did they sometimes occur? 52. How more extensively? 53. How many general persecutions have been enumerated? 54. By what monuments are these statements confirmed? 55. What are the catacombs? 56. How many graves are they estimated to contain? 57. What does this prove? 58. What marks of martyrdom occur on some of the monuments? 59. What did the sufferings of these later victims prove? 60. What respecting the power of their religion? 61. What is said of their imitation of the Savior's prayer? 62. What was the effect of their patience and piety?

Section XXXIV.—1. To what has much attention been devoted? 2. By what have disciples been generally won to Christianity? 3. How has the efficacy of Christianity been proved, in the first place? 4. Why has it not done all that might be desired? 5. What ancient evil custom has it abolished? 6. What of licentiousness and sensuality? 7. What of war and despotism? 8. What account can you give of slavery in ancient times? 9. Of feudal slavery, and the influence of Christianity in destroying it? (See Macaulay's History of England, Chap. I. Remarks on the extinction of villenage.) 10. Of efforts for the removal of modern slavery, and their success? 11. What valuable institutions has Christianity established? 12. What great Christian philanthropists and reformers can you name? 13. How is the efficacy of Christianity displayed in civilizing a rude neighborhood? 14. How in reclaiming a reckless and dissolute man? 15. How in giving comfort to the distressed? 16. How in extending civilization? 17. How can we perceive its influence within ourselves? 18. Name the means through which Christianity influences us indirectly. 19. What is the most powerful evidence to the individual of the truth of Christianity? 20. With what suggestion does the book conclude?

www.ingramcontent.com/pod-product-compliance
Lightning Source LLC
LaVergne TN
LVHW021406110826
845150LV00007B/1801
* 9 7 8 1 4 2 5 5 1 1 8 4 5 *